CHRISTIAN FAMILY

DAVID SECCOMBE

WHITEFIELD PUBLICATIONS

Whitefield Publications

George Whitefield College, P.O. Box 64, Muizenberg 7945, South Africa

6A Almurta Way, Nollamara WA 6061, Australia

www.gwc.ac.za

www.davidseccombe.com

Copyright: © 2020 David Seccombe

Printed by Ingram Spark, Australia, UK and USA.

This book is copyright. Apart from fair dealing for the purposes of private study, research, criticism and review as permitted under the Copyright Act no part of this book may be reproduced by any process without the express permission of the publisher.

Library of Congress Cataloguing-in-Publication Data

Names: Seccombe, David, 1946 – author.

Title: Christian Family / David Seccombe

Description: Cape Town: Whitefield Publications, 2019 | includes footnotes.

ISBN Paperback: 978-0-6398112-0-8

ISBN Mobi: 978-0-6398112-1-5

ISBN Epub: 978-0-6398112-2-2

Subjects: Marriage. | Children. | Family. | Sexuality. | Infant Baptism. | Homosexuality. | Singleness. | Mixed Marriages.

Unless otherwise indicated, Scripture quotations are from the Holy Bible, English Standard Version, copyright © 2001 by Crossway Bibles, a division of Good News Publishers. Used by permission. All rights reserved.

 Created with Vellum

David Seccombe is one of the most stimulating Christian writers I know. This outstanding book on God's purpose for marriage and family not only lays out the Biblical basis for each in a clear, simple and compelling way but it also helpfully tackles many of the most difficult issues. I recommend it highly.

William Taylor, Vicar St Helens Bishopsgate in London

How refreshing it is to read a book that does not tell the reader how to have the perfect Christian family but rather deals sympathetically and honestly with core issues! David Seccombe's book expounds the Bible's teaching with simplicity and clarity, presenting a counter cultural challenge to much contemporary writing on sexuality and what constitutes a family. He deftly unpacks the dire social consequences of ignoring what God has revealed on a broad range of related topics from marriage and family life through infant baptism, homosexuality to singleness. This is an excellent book to distribute to congregations to strengthen their understanding of what families are meant to be. It is also a helpful to dip into "to give an answer for the hope that is in us."

Dr Judith Nichols, Panel Judge, Australian Christian Book of the Year; Women's Worker, St Lawrence's Dalkeith, Western Australia

David Seccombe has produced a reflective and refreshing study of the Christian family in its multi-facetted aspects. The author avoids trite observations and shibboleths but expresses himself by insights that are refreshing and new. The result is vintage Seccombe. *The Christian Family* will be valuable for those intending to get married, those recently married, those who are long-married, and those struggling with same-sex attraction, as well as other expressions of fornication.

Dr Paul Barnett, Former Lecturer at Moore Theological College and Bishop of North Sydney

FOREWORD

David Seccombe's comments on marriage and children should not be overlooked when looking for something to read on this subject. In fact, it should be read first. He has very timely things to say to us all, but more than that, they are true because they are biblical. David always roots all he says and writes in the Word of God. That is who he is and what he has always done. If you want authority, honesty and clarity, read Seccombe. I fervently recommend this little book to you and anybody you know who may be asking these questions.

Dr Frank Retief, Former Presiding Bishop of the Church of England in South Africa

'David Seccombe's book on the family is a profound treatment in a simple and accessible style. In an age when life in families is threatened by intense selfishness, it is essential that we hear again what the Lord has to say to us. I recommend this book for personal reading but also for discussion groups and church gatherings.'

Dr Peter Jensen, Former Principal of Moore Theological College and Archbishop of Sydney

CONTENTS

Why I Wrote this Booklet   vii

1. Christian Marriage   1
2. Children   15
3. The Christian Family   29
4. Family Matters   42
5. Final Word   66

   Notes   73

WHY I WROTE THIS BOOKLET

The family is under fire. Too many families are breaking down. Couples pledge lifelong faithfulness, but when things run rough, are ready to split. Christians make their promises before God and ask his help, but often are unable to hold things together. Children lose out. Some give up on family altogether and seek new arrangements. There is confusion over the very nature of marriage.

I have written this book convinced that God designed marriage and family for human happiness. However, unless we understand what it is, and pay attention to what God has said about making it work, we are unlikely to succeed. I long to see more and more successful families.

I was asked to write a booklet explaining why my Church (Anglican) baptizes infants and children too young to make a considered profession of faith. The Church of England in South Africa, now operating as the Reformed Evangelical Anglican Church in South Africa (REACH South Africa), needed something people could pick up on Sunday, which would explain its position. Baptism of children belongs in the context of family, so I thought it best to look more widely at marriage, children and family.

I also wrote the denomination's policy statement on homosexuality.[1] This was necessary as some churches in South Africa at the time were ordaining practicing homosexuals. As a voluntary association REACH SA had to define its position on certain issues, or face court action if someone took offence at their discipline or refusal of ordination. It had to be in technical language, so it could be used in a court of law. Clearly something simpler was needed for congregation members. I have added a fourth chapter dealing with this and several other troubling issues, in the hope that it will help Christian people with their marriages, inform others of what we believe, and why, and answer some current questions about marriage, family matters and sexuality.

1

CHRISTIAN MARRIAGE

There can hardly be a more important question for the future of human beings and their societies than the true meaning of marriage and family. Are they from God? Or have they evolved by accident? If they are the second, they are ours to do with as we please, and are open to any amount of experimentation and tinkering; the strongest lobby group will decide the future. If they are part of God's creation-design, then we need to tread carefully.

God has given us every reason to know he is real. He has made himself known, along with his plans for the future, and his will for people living in his world. He has done this through prophets, through working close up with a particular nation, through becoming a man, and through apostles and more prophets, who represented Jesus and explained him. All of this is found in the sixty-six books of the Bible. Christians believe that giving us these books was part of God's strategy to reveal himself. The Bible is *his* message. This means that what the Bible says, God says.

It is not as simple, however, as opening to the table of contents and finding the chapter on marriage. Nor will an index help us much. The Bible is the story of God's action in history from the creation of

Adam and Eve to the establishment of his Church, and, in its promises for the future it reaches forward to the coming again of the king of the future world. It was recorded over a period of at least two thousand years, and relates to the life of God's people in very distinct periods. Most important, the Bible itself tells us that the way of life in the period of Israel's commonwealth was intended to be different to that under the new covenant that Jesus would inaugurate by his death. Nevertheless, God's character does not change, and the moral law revealed in the Old Testament remains an essential guide for Christians, even though it needs to be read along with the New Testament.

It is to the Bible, then, that we will go, asking if it provides an answer to the question of marriage. The first thing we discover is that our question is dealt with and answered in Genesis 1-2, the first section of the very first book,. It is clearly a matter of importance.

In a booklet of this length it is not possible to look at everything the Bible has to say about marriage and family. I will choose a few key texts from the Old and New Testaments and try to explain their meaning and relevance. In this chapter we will look at Genesis 2 and Ephesians 5, considering them in their immediate context, but also within the whole matrix of Scripture.

> Then the LORD God said, "It is not good that the man should be alone; I will make him a helper fit for him." Now out of the ground the LORD God had formed every beast of the field and every bird of the heavens and brought them to the man to see what he would call them. And whatever the man called every living creature, that was its name. The man gave names to all livestock and to the birds of the heavens and to every beast of the field. But for Adam there was not found a helper fit for him. So, the LORD God caused a deep sleep to fall upon the man, and while he slept took one of his ribs and closed up its place with flesh. And the rib that the LORD God had taken from the man he made into a woman and brought her to the man.

Then the man said, "This at last is bone of my bones and flesh of my flesh; she shall be called Woman, because she was taken out of Man." Therefore, a man shall leave his father and his mother and hold fast to his wife, and they shall become one flesh. And the man and his wife were both naked and were not ashamed. (Genesis 2.18-25)

Read Genesis 1 and learn where everything came from! It is a big picture of the origin of the physical universe, including energy, matter, time, the world, plants, animals, and finally, humanity. We also learn that humans were created to be somehow like God, and to rule the world for him; we also exist in two forms, male and female, both carrying God's image and sharing his commission. We should keep this in mind as background to our passage.

The surprise that meets us in chapter 2 is that man (Adam) comes first, when we know from chapter 1 that he was the last item in God's creation. Chapter 2 is obviously showing us things from a different angle; humans come first because they are the reason for it all, and the story focuses on one of them in one corner of the world. The climax of chapter 1 is humanity: male and female. It answers the question, "Where do I belong in the cosmos?" The climax of chapter 2 is woman (Eve), marriage and family. It answers questions about the relationship of man and woman. Its position emphasizes its importance; it is found at the beginning of an eleven-chapter staging of the story of God's dealing with the human race.

CONFRONTING loneliness

The problem of loneliness is what meets us first in the words above. God decides that aloneness is not good for the man he has made. We hardly need convincing about this. There are times when we long for solitude, but that is a reaction to overexposure, and is usually temporary. I once conducted a memorial service for a man whose loneliness was so terrible that he hanged himself. As people experiment with short-term relationships, and more and more face old age alone, we can expect that some will find the loneliness too much to bear. God's first provision for the solitary man was the animals. As Adam considers each species and gives it a name, he establishes a relationship with it. Species differs from species, and the kind of friendship I can have with different animals differs. My relationship with a lizard is different to what I can enjoy with a dog or a pet monkey, but even these are not enough to solve the problem.

Superficially it may seem as though God has botched the human design, and then failed to create an animal to rectify his mistake. Could he not have made the man self-sufficient? Could he not have made an animal that could talk and be a friend? But of course, this is just a way of revealing to us the truth about ourselves: we were *designed* to be lonely, designed not to be self-sufficient, and the animals were *intended* not to measure up, because God had something else in mind. God intended that we should not be fulfilled with anything that is not human – and then he makes a helper who corresponds to the man. Some exaggerated forms of Christian spirituality have taught that a relationship with God is all that is needed for complete fulfilment, but this is not the teaching of the Bible, as we see here. We need him, but we also need a human partner.

There is more, of course, to God's provision of a "helper" than just alleviating our loneliness. Together Adam and Eve were to rule over God's creation. This task is now the joint responsibility of the whole human race. A vital part of it is making children and training them up to share in ruling the world. Here the partnership of husband and wife is crucial. We will have more to say about this.

But if it was God's design to make us lonely and needful of an opposite-sex partner, it stands to reason that the first thing we should be thinking about when we contemplate marriage is friendship. We are choosing a friend for life.

WEAKNESS AND STRENGTH

Whoever crafted this story – it is older than Moses – had certainly not observed that men have an uneven number of ribs, or one less than women, or anything like that. We understand that the story is old and the language simple; God inspired the author to write in terms that express his timeless truth to people of all times. The point is that God deprived Adam of a certain kind of strength and added it to the woman. The woman also was deprived of a strength that resides in the man. God designed the man and the woman to be different in a manner that together they would be strong. In whatever way he did it, Genesis tells us the *meaning* of what he did. Woman comes from man, though Paul will later point out that from then on man comes from woman.[1] She shares the image of God, corresponds to him and he to her, but both are different. He has a weakness which makes it difficult for him to be alone. She complements him with strength and provides a solution to his loneliness. We might almost say that together they constitute a whole – though we need to be careful what we mean by this.

MORE THAN A COMPANION

God now brings the woman to the man and he approves. Imagine a young man and a young woman stranded on opposite sides of an island. Suppose they were to survive for a year with no one but the animals. Then one day they meet up on a beach. Imagine the joy! Adam cries out: "This one at last is bone from my bone and flesh from my flesh."

These are curious words! You can imagine them laying the babe on the tummy of a woman who has just given birth to her first child. She exclaims as she sees it for the first time: "This at last is bone from my bone and flesh from my flesh!" It truly is! There may be a clue here: Adam greets Eve as though she is his own flesh and blood. The significance of this becomes clearer in verse 24: "Therefore a man shall leave his father and his mother and stick fast to his wife and they shall become one flesh." What does it mean to be one flesh?

The words are not what we expect. It is common in many cultures for a newly married couple to go to live with the husband's family. The head of that family is usually the husband's father, or even his grandfather. This is a pattern we observe often in the Bible; it seems to have been common in the ancient world, as it is today in many places. Why then does Genesis specify the reverse: the *man* will leave his father and mother and be joined to his *wife*? Perhaps it would be better to ask what effect thinking in the Genesis way will have. There is nothing wrong with a new bride going to live with her husband in a room that he has built in his family's compound. But God wants it to be known that when a man and a woman marry a new family begins. As far as the wife is concerned her husband has left his father and mother to belong now with her – wherever they may choose to live. Her father-in-law or his father is not the head of this family, her husband is. Marriage creates a new family. The Bible does not teach patriarchy. A senior male may be the head of a clan, but a wife belongs with her husband, not to him. "The two shall become one flesh" means the husband and wife are now blood relations; the bond is as close as that of a mother with her newborn child, closer than that of father and son. Your wife or your husband is "bone from your bone and flesh from your flesh." In other words, you are one: blood - relations!

"THE ACT OF MARRIAGE"

In 1976 Tim and Beverley LaHaye published a book with this title. In most people's minds at that time sexual intimacy still belonged with marriage. Sadly this is no longer the case. A former atheist told me that what he saw on television convinced him so deeply that sex outside of marriage was good, that the first question he would put to Christians was what they thought about premarital sex. If they disapproved, he dismissed their Christianity without asking any further question. Happily, he now thinks differently.

Cleaving to your wife or husband and becoming one flesh sounds very like sex, so we should ask here about the place of lovemaking. Adam and Eve had no minister in the garden to marry them, nor a marriage service, nor any set form of words. They married by making love. If there is a God-given sacrament of marriage, it is sexual intercourse. Lovemaking is the outward, visible expression of their inward spiritual bonding. This is one reason extra-marital sex is so disruptive. It is also dishonest.

The joining of a man and a woman and the beginning of a new family is such a significant thing that in all societies ceremonies have developed. It is a sad marriage that begins without the joy of families and friends coming together to mark the moment in some solemn and significant way. However, most societies in their laws also recognize *de facto* marriages where a man and a woman have simply begun to live together. God also may recognize this as true marriage (with or without children); it has come about by a man leaving his mother and father and cleaving to his woman and the two consummating their union sexually. In such a case, leaving one another would be as serious a sin in God's eyes as it would be for a couple with a marriage certificate.

We need to be careful here. The Bible draws a distinction between marriage and fornication. Sex without a commitment to care and be faithful "until death parts us", is against God's will. It is not uncommon for a woman to be drawn into a sexual relationship by pledges of undying love, only to be abandoned at the first sign of difficulty, or when another attractive woman comes on the scene.

The damage that results is serious. Those who wish to please God will avoid such liaisons. Fornication is sin because it causes human misery. If a man and woman are serious about love, they will want the relationship to be tested by engagement, and will not baulk at a ceremony and a pledge of faithfulness before family and friends.

Nonetheless, when couples who are living together approach me for marriage, I do not tell them they are living in sin, though there may have been sin in their original decision to start sleeping together. I tell them that in God's eyes they are already married; what we then talk about is completing, and formalizing, and celebrating their union.

Christians believe in sexual intimacy as "the act of marriage". It is man-woman love expressing itself in a private, passionate, beautiful manner to create an exclusive partnership in life. It is no accident that God also made it to be the act through which a child is conceived and the family grows.

How far we have strayed

Once we grasp these principles we will see how far our modern cultures have strayed from God's pattern. Increasingly in the West, marriage is seen as little more than a romantic friendship. Hopefully it involves that, but in God's plan it is much more. Marriage is the beginning of a new family. I am not thinking here of children. They may follow, or they may not, but they are not essential to the idea of family. The day you marry you become a new family, closer than brother and sister. The friendship you had before marriage will hopefully continue and deepen, but you will fall out at times – perhaps occasionally even feel like you hate each other – just like two brothers, or a daughter and her mother. Close relatives do not for that reason disown each other; there is a bond. Only in a rare and extreme situation might a father expel his son from the family.

Mostly the family goes on – because they recognize that they are flesh and blood relations, who are bonded – for better or for worse. Quality of friendship ebbs and flows, but the family remains. Why then has it become so easy and common for a husband to divorce his wife, or she him? It is because we no longer understand that when we marry we become family.

This is foundational to a Christian understanding of marriage. Jesus referred to Genesis 2 when he said, "What God has joined, do not let human beings separate."[2] Malachi also discusses our passage and says that God hates divorce.[3] So should we. For a married person to divorce his or her spouse is as extreme – more so – than for a person to renounce his mother or father.

The New Testament

If both Malachi and Jesus refer to Genesis 2 and make it foundational to their thinking about marriage, we must have chosen the right Scripture to begin our questioning. But does the New Testament have anything to add? It certainly does! In a passage in which Paul too reflects on Genesis 2 we find out something quite startling.

> Submit to one another out of reverence for Christ - wives, to your own husbands, as to the Lord. For the husband is the head of the wife even as Christ is the head of the church, his body, and is himself its Saviour. Now as the church submits to Christ, so also wives should submit in everything to their husbands. Husbands, love your wives, as Christ loved the church and gave himself up for her, that he might sanctify her, having cleansed her by the washing of water with the word, so that he might present the church to himself in splendour, without spot or wrinkle or any such thing, that she might be holy and without blemish. In the same way husbands should love their wives as their own bodies. He who loves his wife loves himself. For no one ever hated his own flesh, but

> nourishes and cherishes it, just as Christ does the church, because we are members of his body. "Therefore, a man shall leave his father and mother and hold fast to his wife, and the two shall become one flesh." This mystery is profound, and I am saying that it refers to Christ and the church. However, let each one of you love his wife as himself, and let the wife see that she respects her husband. (Ephesians 5.21-33)

The passage is about how married men and women should relate to each other. I will leave the controversial idea of submission for later discussion. If we concentrate on what Paul says here about marriage and Christ's relationship with his church it will push our thinking to a whole new level.

When Paul read our Genesis 2 passage he saw something we don't. He saw Christ! "This mystery (the two becoming one flesh) is great. I am talking about Christ and the Church." How could Paul see Christ and the Church in a passage which is so obviously talking about the marriage of an ordinary man and woman? The first thing that guided him was the way the prophets often likened the relationship between Israel and God to a marriage. At Mount Sinai God entered into a pledged (covenant) relationship with this nation, in which his love and faithfulness were to be reciprocated by their faithful obedience. It is important we understand here that God knows the people he has created. What he told them to obey was not for *his* good, but theirs. By disobeying they would hurt themselves. And especially he created them for friendship with himself; disobedience and unfaithfulness would shatter that relationship – what they were created for. It is crucial we remember this when we consider the analogy between marriage and our relationship with God.

God taught his people to see themselves as a faithful wife. Tragically their union was often marred by rebellious unfaithfulness and "whoring" after other gods. The situation became so extreme that

God announced that he was divorcing them. Yet even as he did this, he promised that one day he would return and woo and marry them once more. Israel's future was to take the shape of a wonderful re-marriage to their God. We learn about this in the book of Hosea.[4]

The second thing that guided Paul was, I think, the discovery of the centrality of Christ to all God's plans and purposes. In the thinking and planning of God, humans and their fall did not come first; Christ did. Before there was an Israel, before there was a rebellion and fall, before there was a man or woman in the image of God, or even a world, God's first thought was Christ (the God-man). God planned that his own Son would become the human king of a race of humans who would share with him in the management and enjoyment of his wonderful creation. It was because of Christ that God made humans in his own image, and because of Christ that he made Adam to be lonely, and because of Christ that he created a complementary person, ("corresponding to him"), and because of Christ that God said, "Therefore a man shall leave his father and mother and join to his wife, and they shall become one flesh." God means marriage to mirror the relationship he intends between Jesus and the people he will save and rule as king. The ultimate destiny of the saved is to be joined to Christ as one family in a bond which is closer than and as personal as that of a husband to his wife.

Of course, I don't think Paul worked this out himself; this is revelation from God, and Christians have always received it gladly. It gives to man, it gives to woman, and it gives to marriage a dignity beyond imagining.

Does Marriage have a Future?

Marriage is under attack. As the Western world has turned away from knowing God, it has placed "democratic society" (or the self) in his place, and is rethinking the whole of life according to what the

"the majority" wants (or I, or the most vocal lobby group, want). Patterns of behaviour which once were seen as contrary to God's will, may now be considered and adopted - if enough people can be persuaded to agitate for them. A huge number of people, young and old, can see no sense in waiting for marriage before sharing a bed, and then marriage may seem superfluous. Those who prefer same-sex partners have now formed an international community and parade their behaviour as commendable and healthy. They agitate for the right to marry - for equality's sake (or respectability's), more than out of a desire to be faithful.

Will marriage survive? We can approach that question sociologically, and look at changing statistics. We will see that marriage is proving quite resilient. That is because it is natural; most cultures have recognized this. God's way accords with our nature. But this is the wrong way for Christians to approach it. We should rather ask what the will of God is. And if we see from Scripture that it is the solemn joining of one man and one woman from different families to become a new family for life, that is what we will practise. Even if we are the only ones who do, we will do it, because we love God and are his people. Our danger is that we lose our nerve and think that because society changes, or the laws change, that we should too. We can be proud to be different: to live God's way. It will not be too many years before the world sees what a terrible mistake it has made. As more and more families are dismantled, the tide of human dissatisfaction will grow. And so will anti-social behaviour. With no God in the world, no ultimate meaning or purpose, no boundaries beyond what a democratic majority decides is best for the moment, why should anyone do what society says? And if every person's way is as good as any other person's preference, can there be a cohesive society at all? Why should a dissenting individual accept what a democratic majority imposes? Why should he not express his anger in some destructive manner? If he feels alienated in the current materialist rat race and wants to feel a sense of purpose, why should he not join a radical group? When we do away with God and his laws we open a Pandora's box of evils.

In marriage we have something precious, something from God, something that teaches us about God, and something to do with the shape of the future. We should not be shy of it, but prize and treasure it, and parade it. A young couple asked me to solemnize their wedding. They were both doctors and told me up front that they were atheists. In answer to my raised eyebrows they assured me that their reason for seeking a Christian wedding was not traditional or cosmetic. They had looked at other ways of getting married, they said, and only the Christian way gave their marriage the sort of significance they felt it had. I suggested that, if there is no God, nothing has any ultimate significance; life is meaningless, and so would their marriage be. They said they understood that, but still it seemed meaningful to them, and therefore they wanted a Christian service.

It may be that our Christian weddings are the last place where we can speak to the unbelieving world, which never comes near a church except for a wedding or a funeral. And is not a wedding the perfect place to speak out the gospel in its beauty and power? Did not God choose a wedding for Jesus to perform his first miracle and manifest his glory?

THE SON of God Reveals his Glory

More often than not when I am asked to give the sermon at a wedding I am drawn to what happened that Tuesday at Cana in Galilee.[5] It was a family wedding to which Jesus' mother had been invited, and Jesus and his disciples went too. It was the groom's responsibility to provide the wine, and it ran out. Mary appealed to Jesus to help. Did she think he would do a miracle? He had never done so before. It had been revealed to her when Jesus was conceived that he would be Israel's king. It must have frustrated her that at the age of thirty he still had made no move in that direction. So perhaps she was thinking that if he were the coming Messiah, this would be a good occasion for him to take some sort of action. Jesus did not think so. He rebuffed her with the words, "My time has not yet come." But it had! The Holy Spirit must have signalled to him that this was the moment to begin "to reveal his glory". God chose a spoiled wedding feast as the place for Jesus to show his hand, because he was moving to fulfil his promise that his broken marriage to Israel would be restored. Jesus ordered the big stone water pots they used for Jewish ceremonial washings to be filled to the brim with water and turned it into the finest wine. What a wedding that must have been! Jesus made a wedding the picture of his coming to earth as the heavenly bridegroom, and an occasion for great celebration.[6]

2
CHILDREN

*C*ompanionship is the first purpose for marrying; the second is children. Genesis 2 implies this in the way it follows the creation of male and female with a general command to "be fruitful and multiply".

> So, God created man in his own image, in the image of God he created him; male and female he created them. And God blessed them. And God said to them, "Be fruitful and multiply and fill the earth and subdue it, and have dominion over the fish of the sea and over the birds of the heavens and over every living thing that moves on the earth." (Genesis 1.27-28)

Humanity's Purpose

In the ancient civilization of Babylon it was believed that humans were created to be the slaves of the gods. Modern materialism views *homo sapiens* as the dominant species, not by divine appointment, but by accident. Pre-Christian Africa saw humans as the creation of

God, but was vague about their purpose. What the Bible reveals is extraordinary; if it were not taught by God himself, it would be beyond belief that humans should be regarded as the image of God and the managers of God's world.

Genesis 2 is brutally frank in identifying the materials out of which we are made as "dirt" ("and to dust you will return"[1]). However, the *design* or *blueprint* is God himself. The truest answer we can give to the question, what is a human being, is that he/she is a representation of God in physical matter in space-time. This breathtaking disclosure is followed by one almost as grand: the purpose of humankind is to rule over the earth and its creatures. The Bible will reveal later that Christ's dominion (and ours) will stretch beyond the earth to the universe, and beyond the universe to embrace even the invisible spiritual powers.[2] The Bible reveals that at creation God intended that humans should even be above the angels. Satan's attack on Adam disrupted this, but our destiny is to reverse our fall. Only God is beyond the mandate of humans to rule. God rules us; we manage the universe. This places us in an amazing situation. When we face God we are dependent creatures, but when we turn to face the world we are like God.

Of course, it was not possible for Adam and Eve to manage the world alone, hence the instruction to "fill the earth". They were to be king and queen of a family of kings and queens. This command to multiply touches us in every generation. Contrary to the antihuman sentiments of some naturists, a depopulated world is not in the interest even of nature. Zambia suffered when whole regions were depopulated as a result of HIV-AIDS. When society broke down in the Sudan as a result of war the animals were hunted almost to extinction. Even national parks need humans to protect and manage them.

However, a general instruction is not a command to every individual; the obligation to develop and maintain a sufficient population is

CHRISTIAN FAMILY

for the human race as a whole. Provided the race is not dwindling, individual couples can choose whether or not to have children and how many. In places where the population is growing out of control it may be a responsible decision to have less children, or none. This choice is part of our mandate to rule.

What is a Child?

It is important that we view our children in the light of our purpose as humans. We do not know all that is entailed in being "the image of God". Certainly it must include everything that qualifies us to manage creation for him. This will include our physical capacities, intellect (rationality), creativity, social and organizational skills, moral awareness, spirituality, and more. In a child all these capacities are in a state of development. We should recognize that our children are potential world-rulers. One of my students was adopted by his mother, but not accepted by her wider family. He was sickly and suffered a serious accident. The family urged his mother to give him away; clearly the ancestors did not want him. But she shielded him and told him not to worry – "one day you will be the president of South Africa", she said. Knowing him now, I think he would be capable of it, if his present job was not more important!

Genesis does not say so, but one would expect that if God has committed the management of his world to human beings and given us an instruction to multiply and fill the earth, he would be interested in the *quality* of our offspring as well as their quantity. Malachi confirms that this is so.

Godly Offspring

> And this second thing you do. You cover the LORD's altar with tears, with weeping and groaning because he no longer regards the

offering or accepts it with favour from your hand. But you say, "Why does he not?" Because the LORD was witness between you and the wife of your youth, to whom you have been faithless, though she is your companion and your wife by covenant. Did he not make them one, with a portion of the Spirit in their union? And what was the one God seeking? Godly offspring! So guard yourselves in your spirit, and let none of you be faithless to the wife of your youth." (Malachi 2.13-15)

Outwardly Israel's service of God seemed alive and well in Malachi's time, but the prophet points out evils under the surface. A number of these touched on the family, as in the present passage about divorce. The easy divorce of that time was practised primarily by men against women. You marry a beautiful young woman, she bears you children, and when her beauty fades you become enamoured with a younger woman and leave "the wife of your youth". In these days of greater independence it is as common for women to leave their husbands. The bottom line is that the covenant of marriage entered into when you were young is put aside by one or the other or both, and the family is shattered. But God was witness, and will hold us accountable for our broken promises. Once again we find Genesis 2 as the subject of reflection. Malachi asks *why* at the beginning God made them one flesh, and the answer is that he was seeking "godly offspring".

It should have been obvious to the Israelites that if God made humans in his own image and entered into relationship with them, and commanded them to be fruitful and multiply and rule his world, that he would want the new generations to know him and be loyal to him. What the Bible reveals, however, is rampant disloyalty. Cain murdered his brother, and the human story is written in blood. God wants godly children, and to this end he commands us to guard our marriages, and to be faithful to the mother of our children.

CHRISTIAN FAMILY

Some of us are old enough to remember a society in which divorce, though possible, was difficult and uncommon. Most children had the security of knowing they had a home, which was theirs, even if it was not a happy home. Today it is not so, and countless children experience the hurt and confusion of a broken home, not knowing where or to whom they belong, and having no experience of normality. We are yet to see whether our societies can hold together in such circumstances.

That is how it is, but we do not have to accept it as normal. Christians are called to live differently. Churches should model a counter-culture, where marriage is treasured – for its own sake, and also for the children's. But there is more to producing godly children than preserving our marriages. If God seeks men and women to rule his creation, how important does that make education and training, both in the family and at school! Isn't it important that children learn how the physical world works? If we are designed to be a reflection of God, yet in a body made from dust, is it not important for children to learn to make the most of their physical bodies - and their minds? And if our rule of the world is in cooperation with others, don't they need to understand how societies work, and about law and politics? And if they are to manage the world for God, don't they need to know what he is like?

If they have any choice, parents should take great care in selecting a school for their children. A church school may not be a good school, or it may. Many church schools do not have a Christian approach to education. A state school with a good head and complement of teachers may be the best you can do. However, schools today are being invaded by anti-Christian philosophies, so care is needed. Visit the school and speak to the head. Get advice from your local church and other parents. Some Christians choose to home school.

SPIRITUAL TRAINING

The way the world is managed will depend on the character of those who make up its populations. This will in turn be heavily influenced by upbringing and education. Final responsibility for a child's education lies with parents. They must decide what they are going to teach their children, and to whom they will entrust them for their further education.

Of first importance is a child's own relationship with God, for this is a matter of life and death. We hasten to teach our children the dangers of hot stoves and deep water; we should also impart the ways of God. Moses saw clearly that Israel's survival as a people under God depended on what parents did with their children.

> Hear, O Israel: The LORD our God, the LORD is one. You shall love the LORD your God with all your heart and with all your soul and with all your might. And these words that I command you today shall be on your heart. You shall teach them diligently to your children, and shall talk of them when you sit in your house, and when you walk by the way, and when you lie down, and when you rise. You shall bind them as a sign on your hand, and they shall be as frontlets between your eyes. You shall write them on the doorposts of your house and on your gates ... When your son asks you in time to come, 'What is the meaning of the testimonies and the statutes and the rules that the LORD our God has commanded you?' then you shall say to your son, 'We were Pharaoh's slaves in Egypt. And the LORD brought us out of Egypt with a mighty hand.' (Deuteronomy 6.4-12)

This kind of training cannot all be done at Sunday School or in a Christian school. That is because the core of it is a relationship of love with the living God. It is *felt* in mother's and father's own love for God, which spills over in many unstudied ways to the children, just as their love (or frustration) with each other will inevitably communicate itself. It is a mistake to think that children must be a certain age before they can understand Christian teaching. Mother and father express their love to their children from the moment they are born – before even. Because your child cannot conceptualize what is happening does not mean he or she is not growing in his or her relationship with you. It is the same with God. You stand in the place of God to your child, and your actions and words flowing from your friendship with God, *are* from him. A child's relationship with God can be nurtured and grow long before it has understanding of that relationship. Understanding grows as the child grows.

Bible Reading and Prayer

I don't think there is any age that is too early for a child to be hearing God's words and participating in the prayers of mother and father. How does a child learn language? Through being spoken to, and hearing the normal conversations of the family! No one thinks a child should understand everything it hears. If God is a member of the family (its head) and is talked about and spoken to, and if his word has an honoured place in our family life, children will grow up to know him. This was the way Moses taught Israel to bring up their children; it is no different now.

The Kingdom of God

The principles of a God-pleasing life set out in the Old Testament for Israel are foundational, and continue to nurture those who fear God today, even where it is clear that his plans for the world have advanced beyond his dealing with one nation. We turn to the New Testament again, therefore, to discover any new insight in the matter of children.

> Now the eleven disciples went to Galilee, to the mountain to which Jesus had directed them. And when they saw him they worshiped him, but some doubted. And Jesus came and said to them, "All authority in heaven and on earth has been given to me. Go therefore and make disciples of all nations, baptizing them in the name of the Father and of the Son and of the Holy Spirit, teaching them to observe all that I have commanded you. And behold, I am with you always, to the end of the age." (Matthew 28.16-20)

This is how Matthew concludes his Gospel; it is how Jesus concluded his sojourn on earth. It says nothing explicitly about children, but includes them, for they belong to the world into which Jesus sends his followers; sometimes they are the most reachable. Jesus begins by declaring his kingship: all authority in the universe is his. He wants the whole world to know this and to come into the safety of his kingdom. Baptism is indicated as the outward symbol of membership, but more important is being led into a disciple–master relationship with the King and being taught the ways of his kingdom. This mission should start with our own children.

What Moses taught Israel will be part of what we teach our children, but now that we live in the new age of the kingdom of God there are important additions and differences. That is why Jesus tells us to teach everything he (the King) has taught; he wants people to know the way into his kingdom, and how to live in it. We are educating and training our children to be able to manage the physical-social-political world, *and* to live the Christian life, *and* to build God's kingdom in the world. Mission should be part of our children's upbringing and training.

Salvation

So far it may appear that if we take good care to educate our children to know God and to understand the world of nature and of humans, they will naturally develop into godly men and women who will do the right thing by his creation and kingdom. Sadly, it is not so simple. This is because of the deep sickness of sin, which affects every person from the moment they are born; it is part of our nature. It is something we inherit from our original parents, so we call it "original sin". Everyone is born with a corrupted nature, that turns away from God and is drawn to rebellion.

Israel failed to keep its law, in part because it neglected its children, but in greater part because of this innate rebelliousness. This is what Jesus revealed. Even the serious practitioners of Moses' law failed in the all-important areas of justice and compassion and love.[3] Jesus told the Jews they were "slaves of sin".[4] If *they* were, how much more are we! What we need is a big forgiveness and a new spirit. This is made very clear in the Old Testament,[5] but Jesus actually made it possible. The crucified king carried the penalty of death deserved by his people and made it possible for God to forgive us without betraying his own justice. Thus reconciled, he comes to live within us through his Holy Spirit. No longer alienated from our heavenly Father, we begin to enjoy the life of his kingdom, which even death cannot destroy. Jesus promises to raise from death everyone who believes in him. All of this and more is what the Bible calls salvation, and Jesus calls on us to turn to God and trust him. He promises salvation as a gift to all who believe, and also to their children.[6]

What Christian parents want most for their children is that they be saved. This is not an inevitable fruit of example and teaching, though both are involved. It certainly does not come through laying down the law, or harsh discipline. Faith comes from the hearing of the gospel. It is not different for children. They too must hear and respond. The gospel is the news of the arrival of God's kingdom through the life, death, resurrection, rule, and coming again of the Lord Jesus. Faith is awakened as the Spirit of God blows through a person's life like the wind, and they are born again. This is supernatural; only God can do it, and for this reason we pray as well as teach. We ask him to do in our children the same miracle he has done for us. We have confidence that he will, though we have no control over it. Nor can we control our children's wills. They will do their own thing, and sometimes break our hearts. All we can do is teach and bear witness, care and pray.

Grace

All I have just said raises an obvious question about the position of children when they are too young to understand and exercise faith. Are children safe until they consciously sin, so they do not need to be saved like we do? Or are they covered by some other provision of God's mercy? Or are they counted as belonging to Christ by virtue of their parent's faith? They are certainly not out of reach of his mercy! On one occasion mothers were bringing their babes to Jesus hoping he would touch them, no doubt to convey a blessing. His disciples, who helped manage the crowds, tried to keep them away. Jesus' reaction does not answer all our questions, but helps us know what to do with our children.

> And they were bringing children to him that he might touch them, and the disciples rebuked them. But when Jesus saw it, he was indignant and said to them, "Let the children come to me; do not hinder them, for to such belongs the kingdom of God. Truly, I say to you, whoever does not receive the kingdom of God like a child shall not enter it." And he took them in his arms and blessed them, laying his hands on them. (Mark 10.13-16)

Jesus was announcing the arrival of the kingdom of God and the twelve apostles were helping. In their minds the kingdom meant a glorious political revolution; they could not see that children had much of a role to play; in the inaugural stages they were a nuisance!

But Jesus knew the kingdom was not to come through political agitation. It will be a kingdom in which every citizen is a friend of God, and will come about as each individual hears the call of the King and surrenders his or her life. This is why he did not raise an army, but preached and taught. He was gathering the citizens of his kingdom. It is highly significant, therefore, that he was glad that children should be brought to him, and blessed them. Mark is vague about the age of the children, but Luke is explicit; they were bringing "even the babies".[7] Jesus rebuked those who would keep them away. "Let the children come to me, and do not hinder them. For of such is the kingdom of God."

Jesus touched and blessed the babies. To dismiss this as sentimentality would be as serious a mistake as the disciples made. He is the King, and, at the very least his blessing means acceptance. To be accepted by the King is salvation. Whatever we do with this theologically – and it raises huge questions – we must not turn our backs on the raw fact that Jesus welcomed babies into his kingdom – and encouraged their parents to bring them to him. Can we bring our children to him today? We can!

Jesus used this occasion to teach an important principle: "Whoever does not receive the kingdom of God like a little child will certainly never enter it." We can rule out innocence as what Jesus is pointing to. None of us can receive the kingdom that way. We can also rule out an understanding faith; babies are not ready for that. Perhaps then, the way a child receives the kingdom has more to do with the King than with the child. Salvation is bestowed as a gift, quite apart from any virtue in the child. It is the same with us. Yes, we understand and believe, but we are mistaken if we think this is a virtue deserving of the kingdom. God bestows his salvation on us out of sheer mercy. True faith is the broken heart that comes to God with nothing –everything it receives is sheer mercy and gift -like a mother's milk to her infant child.

Once we grasp this we can see that when it comes to receiving salvation, the adult and the baby are the same: both are disqualified sinners in need of grace. It raises the possibility of what is sometimes called "prevenient grace".

BACK TO FRONT Grace

The normal way in which salvation works is that we hear the gospel, believe, ask God for his mercy, and he gives it to us – by his grace. This is the pattern the Bible lays out for us in many places. For example, In the famous words of John's Gospel, "God so loved the world that he gave his only Son that whoever believes in him shall not perish, but have everlasting life."[8] However, in the way Jesus dealt with people it did not always happen in that order. People were offended when he dined with notorious "sinners" *before* they had shown any evidence of repentance, because it implied that God accepts sinners.[9] But Jesus' grace towards them *when they were sinners* was the very thing that brought about their repentance. Grace ran before repentance. The truth is, it always does. The Bible makes clear that we are spiritually dead before God's Holy Spirit causes us to be born again.[10] A dead person cannot respond to God's call before being made alive. God's grace works first. He awakens the trust that he then responds to - with forgiveness and the gift of his Spirit. If he does this for an adult, he can do it for a child.

This is the reason some Christians from the beginning have brought their newly born children to Jesus. How can you do this two thousand years on, when he is not physically present? He may not be physically present, but he *is* here. "I am with you every day until the end of the age," he told his followers as he sent them out to baptize and teach. We may bring our children by prayer, asking him to make them his, and bless them. We may also baptize them – or in some churches, which do not like to baptize infants, they may be dedicated. In chapter 3 we will discuss the baptism of infants.

Whose Children?

Children are dependent on others for their very survival. One of the peculiarities of the human race is the helplessness of our offspring in their early years. The dependence of a child on its mother and the bonding that takes place is not accidental; it was designed by God to foster caring community. The mother's care of her child and the husband's care of his wife and protection of the child are all natural, though this arrangement can easily be disrupted. It raises the question to whom a child belongs.

It might seem obvious that children belong to their parents, but which parent? If there is a division between father and mother, does the child belong to one more than the other? Often the state will decide. Does the state therefore have some sort of ultimate ownership? Some modern governments have asserted this. The truth is that children belong to God. We do not create them. We use the term "procreate" meaning we are involved in the act of creation on God's behalf; God gives us a vital role, but it does not establish ownership. Our children belong to God and are entrusted to their parents for nurture and education. If they fail in their exercise of this trust, it may be necessary in extreme situations for the community or state to care for them. This is part of their stewardship, but again it does not establish ownership. Parents may die and children may be adopted. Adopting parents should also realize that they are taking on the care of a child whose owner is God.

There is an important principle to be grasped here, both by carers, and by children as they grow up. If the sovereign God is our true Father, it follows that he chooses whom he will entrust us to for care and upbringing. Usually it will be parents or a parent, but if we are adopted, or raised by the village or placed in an institution by the state, we should accept this as the providence of our loving Father. Children as they grow to discover their true parentage should not think that they are deprived by not having natural parents. It is God's prerogative to decide. Our role, be we parent, grandparent, adopted parent, village, or institution is to shepherd the child in our care to the point where it discovers its true Father. The greatest experience any person can have, surpassing even finding your life partner, is the discovery of your own true Father God, who gave you life, and wants to love you for eternity. To see your children coming to this realization is the greatest joy of parenthood.

CHILDREN MUST HELP

> Children, obey your parents in the Lord, for this is right. "Honour your father and mother" (this is the first commandment with a promise), "that it may go well with you and that you may live long in the land." Fathers, do not provoke your children to anger, but bring them up in the discipline and instruction of the Lord. (Ephesians 6.1-4)

Why does Paul remind us of this commandment and the promise which is attached to it? When Moses gave them God's commandments he knew that Israel's continuance in the promised land would depend largely on what happened in families. Unfaithful marriage partners can shatter a family, but so can children, by disobedience and rebellion. And it is easy for them to be driven to this by heavy-handed fathers (or mothers). "Fathers, do not provoke your children to anger, but bring them up in the discipline and instruction of the Lord." Paul is aware of the need for a delicate balance, which will require great wisdom of mother and father, and cooperation of children. The family is precious; it is the crucible in which the world of the future is being formed.

3

THE CHRISTIAN FAMILY

We have seen how God views our marriages; also how he regards the children of those marriages. We will now consider how he understands families. If the fundamental components of a family are a husband with his wife (the conclusion we drew from Genesis 2) it will be interesting to inquire how much the nuclear family features in the rest of the Bible. At first glance it appears that it does not figure very much; the extended family is what we most see. This reflects the predominant social reality of the ancient world, which makes Genesis 2 all the more surprising. So how are we to think of the family? There are two examples I would like us to consider, one from the Old Testament and one from the New.

ABRAHAM AND SARAH

Terah took his family, which included Abraham and his wife Sarah, and nephew, Lot, and servants – so it was an extended family – and they moved from Ur in southern Iraq to Haran in Eastern Turkey. It was there that God spoke to Abraham and told him to leave his father and strike out alone: "Leave your country, your people, and your father's household and go to the land I will show you." Abraham set off with "his wife, his nephew, Lot, and the people they had acquired in Haran." This is the family that is going to determine the future history of the world. Essentially it is a man and his wife and their future children. But there is also a nephew and servants, who are regarded as part of the household, but will come and go as circumstances change. Abraham's heir initially was Eliezer, a slave born in the household, but he hardly figures in the unfolding story.[1] Hagar bears a surrogate child for Sarah, but she and Ishmael also fade from view.[2] It is the man and his wife that stand central. If you read the story in Genesis, you will notice how often God acts to protect Sarah's position. *She* is the wife and *she* will bear the promised son. The essential family is the man and his wife, and any children they may bear or adopt. A child belongs to the family until he or she goes off to form a new family. And now we observe that when God called Abraham, that call extended to his nuclear family. They travel together and make a home together. God viewed them and treated them as a unit.

Joseph and Mary

The second example – from the New Testament – is that little story about Jesus going with his family to Jerusalem when he was twelve years old.[3] Again it is the extended family, which first meets the eye. Mary and Joseph do not travel alone; they make the journey with a sizable party of relatives and friends – enough of them for a child to get lost in, and not be in danger, but also not be missed. And yet, when they discover that Jesus is not with the party, it is Joseph and Mary - father and mother - who are responsible for their son. It is they who experience the anguish, and must leave the party and go back to Jerusalem. Again we see the fundamental reality of the nuclear family.

Mary reacts like many mothers who have lost a child, and then found it: her relief at finding the boy safe in the temple is mixed with anger at his thoughtlessness. Jesus' reply is the reason Luke tells the story: "Didn't you know that I had to be in my Father's house?" You could read this as a jibe against Joseph, who of course is not Jesus' biological father, but I don't think it is. Joseph is his real, legal father - by adoption; Luke and Matthew are both clear about that.[4] But Jesus knows that in the truest sense his father is God. Of course, he is the only begotten Son of God, but we have seen that it is also true for us, that we are not owned by our parents, but by our Creator, who wishes to become our Father. This makes the sequel to this story all the more significant.

Jesus goes back to Nazareth with his parents and is "submissive" to them.[5] That word is the same as in Ephesians 5.22 where wives are urged to cooperate with the leadership of their husband. God, his true Father, places him under the authority of a human father and mother. Jesus honoured his mother and his father according to the commandment;[6] he accepted their leadership and was obedient to them.

The Family Commandments

Three of the Ten Commandments establish the idea of family. Children are commanded to honour their father and mother, adultery is forbidden, and men are commanded not to covet another person's wife.

> Honour your father and your mother, that your days may be long in the land that the LORD your God is giving you. (Exodus 20.12)

Father and mother are equally honoured. There is no disrespect of women in the foundation documents of Judaeo-Christianity, quite the opposite. A child is called to be obedient to both. He or she is not commanded to obey grandparents or brothers or sisters or uncles. They may, of course; respect for elders is good, but obedience is not commanded and will depend on what mother and father say. In the Book of Proverbs we find wisdom for living a successful life. It is notable how highly this book esteems the guidance of a mother and a father.[7]

BAPTIZING FAMILIES

Turn now to Acts 16 to observe something very interesting in the way early Christianity approached the family. In Acts 16.13-15 we meet Lydia, the Jewish cloth merchant from Thyatira, whom Paul met and evangelized at a riverside place of prayer in Philippi.

> The Lord opened her heart to pay attention to what was said by Paul. And after she was baptized, and her household as well, she urged us, saying, "If you have judged me to be faithful to the Lord, come to my house and stay." And she prevailed upon us. (Acts 16.14-15)

Lydia does not appear to have a husband, but she does have a family. A "house" is the word Luke uses; it means a household or family. When she hears the gospel from Paul, and God opens her heart, she is baptized along with her household. We don't know what that household consisted of, but it seems that Paul viewed it as a unit. The head of the household made the decision to follow Christ, and the family followed. Whether all agreed with Lydia's decision and entered into personal faith we are not told. But the family is now regarded as belonging to Christ. I suppose someone could leave the family, but for the time that they remained they were part of a baptized household, and thus regarded as a Christian family. We might overlook this as just a curiosity, if we didn't encounter something similar in the same city in the case of the

CHRISTIAN FAMILY

keeper of the prison where Paul and Silas were held. An earthquake broke open the cell doors and the distraught jailer was only prevented from suicide by Paul's reassurance that no one had escaped.

> Then he brought them out and said, "Sirs, what must I do to be saved?" And they said, "Believe in the Lord Jesus, and you will be saved, you and your household." And they spoke the word of the Lord to him and to all who were in his house. And he took them the same hour of the night and washed their wounds; and he was baptized at once, he and all his family. Then he brought them up into his house and set food before them. And he rejoiced along with his entire household that he had believed in God. (Acts 16.30-34)

Paul's answer to the jailer's plea for salvation included his family (household). He assumes that holding out the promise of salvation to the head of the household is tantamount to offering it to the whole family. We learn next that the whole household was baptized. Luke emphasizes the fact by noting it four times.

> "Believe in the Lord Jesus Christ and you will be saved – *you and your household."*

> "Then they spoke the Word of the Lord to him *and the others in his house."*

> "The immediately he *and all his family* were baptized."

> "The jailer ... was full of joy because he had come to believe in God – he *and his whole family."*

Once again, we don't know who was in that family, but a working jail superintendent might be expected to have a wife and any number of children, as well as servants and other extended family.

The family is assumed to be a solidarity extending all the way to the baptism of the whole, which will now be identified as Christian, even though we may speculate that not all of them were born again, nor yet had a real relationship with Christ.

Infant Baptism

Anglicans and most of the old denominations follow the practice of the ancient churches in baptizing infants. At the time of the sixteenth century Reformation there was a protest against this by so-called Anabaptists ("re-baptizers"). In those days almost everyone in Europe was baptized and belonged to the church, yet many showed no signs of having a relationship with God. The Anabaptists required an adult profession of faith and an adult baptism. Mennonites and Amish are two current traditions that come from this movement. Other denominations which do not baptize babies, like the Baptists, and the Churches of Christ, and Pentecostal denominations came later. It is not possible to *prove* from Scripture that babies were baptized in the apostolic church, and the New Testament neither commands nor prohibits it, so it is understandable that Christians will have different views, and that denominations will follow different practices. It is not an issue that should hinder Christian fellowship, though it has inevitably led to different traditions and families of churches (denominations).

It seems to us in the Anglican tradition (to which REACH South Africa belongs) that the weight of the evidence shows that the early church baptized whole families including young children and babies. Article 27 of the Thirty Nine Articles says, "The Baptism of young Children is in any wise to be retained in the Church, as being most agreeable with the institution of Christ." At the same time, we recognize the problems that led to the protest, and try to address these in our own way.

• • •

FAMILY SOLIDARITY

From beginning to end the Bible bears witness to the solidarity of the family in the eyes of God. A family is a collection of distinct persons and each will be judged individually. Nevertheless, they make up a unity that is part of the plan and purpose of God. This unity is what makes baptism of babies appropriate, but it is much bigger than just a justification for baptism.

Think of what it must have been like to decide for Christ back then! Whether he meant to or not, a man was making a decision that would affect his whole family. If there is persecution, it will not stop at him; it will affect his wife and children. Conversely, the blessing which comes to someone who turns to God, will be felt by the whole family. God has always respected the solidarity of the family. Abraham's family travelled with him and shared his sufferings as well as his blessing. We could note in passing that by God's command Abraham's male children were circumcised, though not all of them turned out to be spiritual people.

In 1992 I was asked to go to South Africa to teach at George Whitefield College. The country was still in turmoil as the struggle to end apartheid concluded. It was unthinkable that Lorraine and I would not act together; we were husband and wife. But what we decided would also affect the children. I put it to our three children at the breakfast table in terms of a choice: none of us could go, or we could all go, or Mother and I could go, and "you children could go to boarding school." I put this last one in to see the effect; I don't know what we would have done if they had chosen it. But the eldest, aged eight, responded immediately: "Dad, whatever we do, we are staying together." Of course, they had no idea of the dangers we were going to face (neither did we). They came because they were part of the family. There is a mysterious solidarity about the family: it lives together, moves together, is blessed together and suffers together. That is how God means it to be.

It is for this reason that it is right to talk about a Christian family. Baptism is the sacrament of entry into Christian faith and the Church, which is the visible embodiment of Jesus' kingdom at the present time. Children belonging to a Christian family may therefore be baptized and recognized as church members.

ARE CHILDREN SAVED BY BAPTISM?

There are some difficult questions relating to the baptism of infants, which, historically, have given rise to different answers. Does baptism save? Scripture is very clear that *it does not*. We are saved by grace, through faith, and faith is the gift of God; it is not initiated by our striving, nor is it tied indissolubly to a church administered rite.[8] The sacrament of baptism is the outward, visible sign of faith and forgiveness. For a person of understanding baptism signifies their turning to Christ and the washing away of their sins by Jesus' atoning death. For a child in solidarity with the family it is a prayer for and anticipation of God's forgiveness. Two thousand years of history and common experience has shown that baptized people do not always turn out to be people of faith. It is not right therefore to tie regeneration to baptism, as though it were automatic. Article 27, On Baptism", is sometimes misunderstood. The first part of the article is about "Christian men" (i.e. adults) and speaks about the primary meaning of baptism. It says that baptism, rightly received, is a sign of new birth, and a kind of legal "instrument" by which a person receives church membership.

> Baptism is not only a sign of profession, and mark of difference, whereby Christian men are discerned from others that be not christened, but it is also a sign of Regeneration or new Birth, whereby, as by an instrument, they that receive Baptism rightly are grafted into the Church; the promises of forgiveness of sin, and our adoption to be the sons of God by the Holy Ghost, are visibly signed

CHRISTIAN FAMILY

and sealed; Faith is confirmed, and Grace increased by virtue of prayer unto God." Thirty Nine Articles 27

Notice that in baptism "faith is confirmed". The assumption is that an adult coming for baptism does so because he or she already believes, and is therefore already saved. Otherwise the baptism is not "rightly received". Baptism visibly signs and seals a faith which already exists, and in the process builds our faith and increases God's grace to us.[9]

Children's baptism is mentioned only at the end of the article as "agreeable with the institution of Christ". The meaning we give to it will be significantly different to what we give to adult baptism, because regeneration is a work of God's Holy Spirit, which takes place in his time. Jesus explained, "The wind blows where it wills; you hear its sound, but and you do not know where it comes from or where it goes. So it is with everyone who is born of the Spirit."[10] There is something mysterious here: something within the control of the sovereign God alone. There is no promise that God will answer our prayers for our children immediately, nor that he will oblige with his Spirit during the ceremony of baptism. All we can do is ask him, bring our children to baptism, and raise them "in the training and instruction of the Lord".[11] The meaning of the infant baptism service focuses on believing prayer for God to do his work, and signifying the benefits that will follow – with an important addition.

In the Anglican service for the baptism of infants, parents and godparents are asked to profess faith for the child. It is on the basis of this profession that the child is baptized and received into "the congregation of Christ's flock" (the Church). This sounds strange, but given all we have discovered about the solidarity of the family, is the best way to sign and signify a child's true status. You could say the baptism service is a piece of drama: the child's faith is enacted on its behalf, and on the basis of this faith the promises of the gospel are declared. The baptized child is recognized as a member of Christ's Church and taught to live up to that privilege.

CHRISTIAN CHILDREN

> Children, obey your parents in the Lord, for this is right. "Honour your father and mother" (this is the first commandment with a promise), "that it may go well with you and that you may live long in the land." Fathers, do not provoke your children to anger, but bring them up in the discipline and instruction of the Lord. (Ephesians 6.1-4)

Here is a clear instruction to parents to train their children in the ways of God. But how is this done? Do we regard our children as enemies of God until such time as they can profess faith? Or do we treat them as his children – until such time as they reject him? It is unthinkable that parents would not include their babies and small children in their own relationship with the Saviour. This is evident in the way we pray with them: we include them in our family prayers, and teach them to pray to God as their own heavenly Father. We do not keep them at arms-length as though they do not belong until they have done something adult. We bring them to Jesus in the way he said, and assume his acceptance of them.

Small children naturally do as their parents say and accept what their parents model. If mother tells them to believe in Jesus they will do as she asks. This means that up to the age of adolescence we are likely to hear many expressions of faith from our children, but may not know how real they are. It is only as a child enters its years of questioning, critical reflection, and testing that the true condition of its heart will emerge. Even here we must be careful. It is part of natural adolescent development to challenge things – this is not sin. Also, when dealing with our children we should never forget that they, like us, are sinners. A child of God is not someone who is never disobedient or rebellious. Final judgements on a person's status with God are best left with God and with the person themselves.

Exhortation

As children grow in their ability to understand, we should explain to them the importance of having their own faith in the Lord Jesus. They cannot forever coast on the faith of their parents, or presume on their church membership: they must turn to God personally and have a faith of their own. A presumption of faith is often reinforced in churches which treat all their members as Christians and cease to preach the gospel. It can lead to what we call nominalism: baptized church members who feel secure in being Christian but do not have a personal faith. The Bible has many warnings against this, so we need to beware of the possibility.[12] A church in which the gospel is kept central, and the call to conversion often heard will be helpful to Christian parents bringing up children. It is not uncommon that a child raised by faithful parents and exposed to a gospel-preaching ministry will respond with a profession of faith on more than one occasion – or many. Looking back in later life they may identify one decisive moment as their "conversion". This is fine, so long as we keep in mind that the real motive power is God's, and that ultimately only he knows the when and the how.

Confirmation

In the Anglican tradition there is a ceremony in which a person who has been baptized as a baby can publicly own the Christian Faith as his or her own. Confirmation is not "a sacrament of the gospel" like baptism and the Lord's Supper. These two are commanded by Jesus. Confirmation is a ceremony designed to mark an important movement into adult Christian life. As with all rites and ceremonies this can become an empty ritual, a "rite of passage", part of growing up in a Christian society. But properly stewarded by careful parents and a faithful church, it can be an important time for a young Christian to explore whether they want to commit themselves to a lifetime of following Jesus. Care must be taken not to push it on young people. Churches should never have an accepted age for confirmation that will place psychological pressure on young people to conform. There should, of course, be a normal minimum age. It is unwise in my view for confirmation to take place in early adolescence. This is when a young person is least stable. Confirmation is not to be thought of as a way to strengthen wavering or uncertain young people. We do not want to set them up to make professions of faith they will later go back on. Seventeen or eighteen is a more sensible age when people are emotionally ready to make a life commitment. Parents should never pressure their children to confirmation. This is their child's moment to testify; it should be for them to decide when they want to do it.

Doing Family

At this point we should be thinking about how to succeed at being a family. I don't feel qualified to advise on that subject. I have four children, all of them grown up and following Christ. I do not attribute that to their upbringing alone, but to the grace of God. In many ways, as I look back, it seems like it was hit and miss, with a lot of misses. One thing is for sure, Lorraine and I prayed for those children to know God from the moment they were born, and before. And God has been kinder than we dared to hope. Seeing their own faith flower, some of them only well into adulthood, has been the greatest joy of our life.

From when they were little we read the Bible together, and prayed as a family, and that continued all the time we had them with us. We read other books. and did lots of stuff together. I had a principle -

CHRISTIAN FAMILY

whatever I was doing - of taking a child with me whenever I could. Nursing homes became familiar places. Precious are the memories of picnics, camping holidays, and beach missions. We were also part of a church, which has been hugely important. When children of Christians go to school they soon discover that Mum and Dad are different. Christianity is strange to most of their friends. It is natural to pull away from the family's faith. But an active church, and older people they relate to positively make it clear that their parents are not so weird. "So-and-so believes in Jesus and he or she is a cool person, who I like." How important it is that churches take seriously their responsibility to children and make Sunday a good day! How important that they teach from time to time on family issues and organize family events!

There are helpful books to assist with ideas for making family work, but just remember that every family is different – like every individual – and there is no formula. Follow the guidance of God's Word, not just about family, but about relationships generally: practice love, justice, truth, patience, forgiveness and all the fruits of the Spirit - with your children - and know that God will work with you. Your children belong to him and he loves them – as he loves you and is working in you to make you like Jesus. Learning to live and work with your children is part of *your* learning to follow Christ. You are not alone; the God who is Father, Son and Holy Spirit is with you. My eldest daughter's story is included as an appendix at the end of this book.

4

FAMILY MATTERS

*J*n this last chapter we will attend to some common questions that arise when thinking about marriage and family. What happens to children who die before making a decision to follow Christ? What if a young person, who was baptized as a child, wants to be baptized as an adult? If marriage is normal, how should we view people who remain single? Does it matter if I marry outside of my faith? What is the place of lovemaking in marriage? Is a Christian woman required to be subordinate to her husband? How does God view homosexuality? Is divorce always wrong? Is remarriage after divorce allowed in the Bible? These are the questions I will deal with, though there are many more.

YOUNG CHILDREN

We have been talking about children, so we begin with what happens to a child who dies in infancy. This is a question the Bible does not answer directly, so we need to be careful. Some Christians believe all children are safe until they commit actual sin. This may be true, but it ignores the fact that everyone is born sin-*ful*, whether or not they have had the chance to express it. Theologians speak of "original sin" meaning that we inherit a sinful nature through our membership of the family of Adam and are born into a humanity which is under God's judgement. The very fact that children die is proof of that. So, children need to be saved, even the tiniest babes.

Roman Catholics and many others believe children are saved by baptism. That is why, in hospitals, when a baby's life is in danger a nurse may sometimes carry out a baptism – with the Church's blessing. But it claims too much for a human ceremony, and goes against much that the Bible teaches to think that salvation can be had by means of an outward ritual. If it were true that eternal life could be gained for a child simply through baptizing them, we would expect the New Testament to have given explicit instructions for it, but it does not.

The Bible promises salvation to those who put their trust in Jesus. A small child cannot do this, but we have seen that God treats the family as a unit. A parent's faith, therefore, may cover their child. If the child dies young, Christian parents may be confident that God will look after their child, just as he has saved them. There is another way of looking at this. You can bring your child to Jesus, just as parents did the time when Jesus intervened to stop the disciples sending them away. That he, the King, blessed their babies and spoke of the kingdom belonging to them shows that he extended the gift of salvation to them. If one of these children was ill (like Jairus's daughter), Jesus healed it, and it would have grown up to know him. This gives us confidence to believe that if we sincerely and prayerfully bring a dying child to Jesus today, he will save it and raise it up at the resurrection to be the person he intends. We don't need to think it will stay a baby – the resurrection is the great healing and perfecting of God's creation, when all will reach their perfect potential.

When I was chaplain to a women's hospital I was once called out after midnight to baptize a newborn who was not expected to live. The parents were distraught and wanted to do anything to help their little one. I could not tell them that baptism would save their child. I could not comfort them with the fact that they were children of God, and therefore their child was safe, because they gave me no reason to think they were. What could I say? I read to them from Mark 10. I explained that if they had lived when Jesus was on earth, they could have taken their child to him and he would have healed it and welcomed it into his kingdom. I told them they could do that now by coming to him themselves in simple faith – with their babe. On that understanding we shared together in baptism. I had every confidence that Jesus would respond to their faith, if it was real. Whether it was, I had no way of knowing. What the future of the child was, if it was not, I do not know. The Bible does not answer all our questions. The one thing we can be sure of is that God responds to faith, and he holds the faith of a parent to cover their child. So, we should not hesitate to bring our children to Jesus. Baptism is the obvious formal way of doing this. It not only gives us a way to declare our faith and request the Lord's blessing for our child, it also allows God's promise of salvation to be declared and heard. If for some reason baptism is not possible, or we belong to a denomination that discourages the baptism of small children, we may still bring our child to God with prayer and know that it will be accepted.

As a minister I sometimes meet new Christians who wish to be baptized as adults, though they were "christened" as children. Some feel their original baptism was illegitimate because their parents did not hold the faith, others feel deprived of something they think would be meaningful to them. Re-baptism has a history and at times has been regarded with great disapproval. In most mainline denominations it is not permitted, as it seems to question the validity of baptism itself. However, we can understand the feelings of those who think otherwise. To deal with this pastorally I have explained that people are saved by faith, not baptism, and that they can *own* their original baptism (as I have my own), even if there was something questionable about the way it was done or received. Baptism, after all, is the sign of something, not the reality itself. But I have no objection to people "re-enacting" or reaffirming their baptism, much as some couples wish to reaffirm their marriage vows. Sometimes I include them in a public baptism of others and allow them to come with me into the river.

Singleness

We have seen that God instituted marriage as a remedy for loneliness, as well as the appointed means of having children and propagating the race. This raises the question of how we are to view singleness. Some people choose it, others would love to have a life partner but things do not work out for them. And today, of course, we can hardly avoid the situation of the person with "same-sex" inclinations.

Christianity does not view singleness as an inferior state, for the simple reason that Jesus himself chose not to marry. It should surprise us that Jesus did not marry, when we realize how often Genesis 2 was in his thoughts. There must have been other principles in play to prevent him doing what was expected and normal in the society of his day.

> The disciples said to him, "If such is the case of a man with his wife, it is better not to marry." But he said to them, "Not everyone can attain to this saying, but only those to whom it is given. For there are eunuchs who have been so from birth, and there are eunuchs who have been made eunuchs by men, and there are eunuchs who have made themselves eunuchs for the sake of the kingdom of

heaven. Let the one who is able to attain this attain it." (Matthew 19.10-12)

Jesus had declared divorce and remarriage to be tantamount to adultery, except in the case of "fornication". His followers regard this as so difficult that they suggest it would be best to refrain from marriage altogether! It is to this thought that Jesus responds. Clearly, he views a decision not to marry as a serious option - but not for everyone. I doubt he means to be taken literally when he mentions eunuchs. A eunuch was a man without testicles, a common thing in the ancient world, where slaves were sometimes castrated so they could safely be given the care of women and girls. However, it was not so common in Jewish society as would explain this saying. Jesus is probably using a vivid metaphor to refer to the person who lives without a sexual partner. Some are born this way, some are so because of what has been done to them, and some choose it. The first two cases we can explain in terms of the Fall; the world is in an imperfect state, we must live with much that we would wish was different. The third case is special. He holds out the possibility that someone might choose to forego marriage for the sake of the kingdom of God. We are moving from a state in which the world is fallen to a new world "where righteousness dwells", and the transition entails much conflict. Jesus had a mission. He understood himself to be locked in a struggle with "the prince of this world" (Satan). He knew it would lead to his death, and along the way he would have to turn his back on family ties, even treating his own mother as though he hated her.[1] Little wonder that he opted not to marry. So, the single life – consecrated to the cause of the kingdom – is also "an honourable state of life". But Jesus is clear that it is only for those who can handle it. The word he uses (*choreo*) means to reach as far as something. His assumption is that most cannot reach this far. But many have chosen, and still choose, to devote themselves exclusively to Christian ministry, and Paul also commends it, albeit for those who are able.[2]

CHRISTIAN FAMILY

So, what is the state of a single person? They are hardly family-less, since they may have parents and belong to a family, perhaps with brothers and sisters (as Jesus had), and nieces and nephews and whatever else. We should treasure this. Singles, more than marrieds, are sometimes able to give time to the wider family. Unmarried aunts and uncles can be an important glue across the generations. And in addition to their blood relations there is also the Christian family. Think of Jesus, who loved Lazarus and his sisters and was always welcome in their home; or Paul, who appears to have found a home and close fellowship with the Jewish traders, Aquila and Priscilla. Christian families should open themselves to include singles in their fellowship. The local church should view itself as an extended family and provide a real home for all its members. In its preaching it should not *presume* that everyone is married or on the way to marriage.

Mixed Marriages

I was once seated in an aeroplane with a young Jewish woman, who, in the midst of our conversation said to me, "Look I am a Jew, but I'm not strict - but my mother is strict! My boyfriend is a Dutch Reformed Christian, and he's not strict - but *his* mother is strict! Do you think our marriage will work?" As I began to answer her question, a young man in front appeared over the top of the seat to ask whether he could listen in. It turned out he also was Dutch Reformed, and had a mother who was strict. We spent quite a bit of the journey talking about mixed marriages. For both of them it was an emotional question, especially for the Jewish girl. Malachi addressed the Jews of his day on this question, and unfolds a principle which applies to Jews and Christians.

> Have we not all one Father? Has not one God created us? Why then are we faithless to one another, profaning the covenant of our

fathers? Judah has been faithless, and abomination has been committed in Israel and in Jerusalem. For Judah has profaned the sanctuary of the LORD, which he loves, and has married the daughter of a foreign god. May the LORD cut off from the tents of Jacob any descendant of the man who does this, who brings an offering to the LORD of hosts! (Malachi 2.10-12)

This is the passage that goes on to talk about godly offspring. But another of the sins of his day, which Malachi put his finger on, was marrying outside the covenant (Jewish) family. The Old Testament in clear. God was in a special relationship with the people of Israel, and has bound them to himself in an exclusive marriage-like relationship of worship and service. For them to marry someone who worshipped another god was forbidden. Gentiles were regarded as unclean, which reinforced the separation. The exception was when a foreigner turned to worship Israel's God – like Ruth the Moabitess. In practice this meant marrying a fellow Jew. Jewish people to this day take this very seriously.

So how is it for Christians? Jesus made it clear that from the time of the crucifixion all nations would be clean. There is now no racial restriction on whom Christians may marry. In South Africa this was once a very contentious issue because the Bible's teaching was twisted, making it a crime to marry "across the colour-line". This reinforced an old evolutionary idea about keeping bloodlines pure.[3] Thankfully this has now ceased to be believed. There is a sense of freedom, and many Christians of varying ethnic backgrounds are falling in love and marrying. There may be cultural differences which make marriage difficult, but there is no barrier on the ground of ethnicity.

Nevertheless, for a believer to marry someone who does not share their commitment to serve and worship the true God is most unwise. The New Testament is as negative about a believer marrying an unbeliever, as the Old Testament was for the Jews.

> Do not be unequally yoked with unbelievers. For what partnership has righteousness with lawlessness? Or what fellowship has light with darkness? What accord has Christ with Belial? Or what portion does a believer share with an unbeliever? What agreement has the temple of God with idols? For we are the temple of the living God; as God said, "I will make my dwelling among them and walk among them, and I will be their God, and they shall be my people. Therefore, go out from their midst, and be separate from them, says the Lord, and touch no unclean thing; then I will welcome you, and I will be a father to you, and you shall be sons and daughters to me, says the Lord Almighty." (2 Corinthians 6.14-18)

It is not clear what relationships Paul had in mind when he wrote these words. Probably he was addressing the problem of unbelieving false teachers coming into the church at Corinth and winning the people over to their way. Nevertheless, the passage establishes a principle which applies to marriage. A marriage in which two people with different value systems are joined together is an unequal yoking; they will pull each other in different directions and cause much friction. Nowhere will this be more apparent than in the bringing up of children.

Roman Catholics are seriously against intermarriage, not across ethnic lines, but with people of other church denominations. Perhaps they do not enforce it as they once did; too many of their people have ignored it. But logically, if you believe that you are the one true Church, and that those who belong to God are those who belong to your church, then the Bible's teaching will mean you don't marry outside of your own denomination. It is interesting to note that Muslims also take this principle very seriously; Muslims must marry Muslims. Most Christians know we don't belong to a chosen national group; nor do we believe our denomination is the only true church. So, we are free to marry whomever we choose – "only in the Lord".[4] Marrying "in the Lord" means marrying a fellow believer.

More than this, if we are wise, we will be careful to marry a Christian who shares our values - for the sake of our worship and service of God, and because we know it is his will that we establish a Christian family and raise "godly offspring". A question a couple contemplating marriage could ask is whether they can pray together to the God who is Father, Son and Holy Spirit.

This is what I tried to explain to my two new friends somewhere over the Great Karoo. I couldn't speak for the mothers, but from God's side, I said, it did not matter whether they were Jew or Gentile, or Dutch Reformed or Roman Catholic. But if they loved God - and that means loving his Son - they should marry someone who shares that relationship. If their religion is only formal, it hardly matters whom they marry. In that respect one unbeliever is the same as another.

LOVEMAKING in **Marriage**

Many books have been written to help in this delicate area. Help is needed because real lovemaking is not as easy as we dream. Explicit movie scenes make it look like heaven is to be had here on earth, in bed, a day or two after a couple first meet. This is a fantasy; among other evils it is calculated to leave ordinary people wondering if they are normal, or whether they have chosen the right partner.

The idea that prior sexual experience will help a marriage is a myth. Firstly, there is the obvious danger of bringing disease into the partnership. In some parts of the world one partner's previous adventures can be a death sentence for their spouse. Two people who forego prior sexual experience and are faithful to each other in their marriage create a haven of shelter from sexually transmitted infections, including HIV and AIDS.

Second, entering marriage imagining we have some prowess can set the new relationship off on the wrong foot; far better that husband

CHRISTIAN FAMILY

and wife are both without experience and can explore their new sexual relationship as equals. How horrible it can be for a man or woman to be wondering whether they are "as good" as the previous partner! Sensitivity to the partner's feelings is the best guide. Sexual intimacy is about two people dropping all the barriers and *knowing* - or better, *learning to know* each other. "Knowing" is the word the Bible often uses to describe lovemaking. It demands a level of communication which is more than physical. What does the Bible tell us?

> Now concerning the matters about which you wrote: "It *is* good for a man not to have sexual relations with a woman." But because of the temptation to sexual immorality, each man should have his own wife and each woman her own husband. The husband should give to his wife her conjugal rights, and likewise the wife to her husband. For the wife does not have authority over her own body, but the husband does. Likewise, the husband does not have authority over his own body, but the wife does. Do not deprive one another, except perhaps by agreement for a limited time, that you may devote yourselves to prayer; but then come together again, so that Satan may not tempt you because of your lack of self-control. Now as a concession, not a command, I say this. I wish that all were as I myself am. But each has his own gift from God, one of one kind and one of another. (1Corinthians 7.1-7)

The Corinthian Christians wrote to Paul seeking his guidance on sexual and other matters. Perhaps they suggested it is spiritually superior not to touch a woman – even in marriage – and Paul is seeming to agree with them, but then making it clear that celibacy is only for a few, and that normal sexual relations in marriage are good. He knows that unrealistic ideas about not touching your spouse will soon lead to touching others! In light of the rest of the letter, however, and the notoriously promiscuous society of Corinth, it is more likely that they are asserting: "It is not good for a man *not* to touch a woman." This is more like the mentality of many today, who see abstention as psychologically damaging. Paul contradicts them: "It *is* good for a man not to touch a woman, but because of temptation let each man have his own wife, and each wife her own husband."

This is not to be read as though the sole purpose of marriage is the avoidance of sexual temptation. We have seen Paul's high view of marriage. Rather it is to understand that there was a very real problem of promiscuity in Corinth, as there is everywhere. Many of the temples were supported financially by the proceeds of prostitution, both hetero- and homo-sexual. Unrealistic ideas about celibacy, as much as animal notions of sex as a bodily necessity, laid the Corinthians open to indulging in sex outside of marriage. We should be realistic about the fact that regular sexual relations between a husband and wife reduce the temptation to indulge elsewhere. Let me state this differently: a husband depriving his wife, or a wife holding out on her husband can lead to consequences as serious as an affair, going to a prostitute, or even child abuse.

Paul gives men and women absolutely equal rights when it comes to lovemaking. In this respect the husband does not own his own body, his wife does! Of course, this does not mean coercion; he is exaggerating to make the point: when it comes to sex a husband should willingly surrender himself to his wife's will, and vice versa. This is what love is. Each sees themselves as there for the other. To go into sex with the motive of self-gratification is to kill it. The beauty of lovemaking is seeking and sensing the pleasure of your partner. We should learn from this passage that lovemaking in marriage is normal and good, and a means to minister to one another in love. It has been well said that the two most spiritual aspects of marriage are praying together and making love.

SUBMISSION

CHRISTIAN FAMILY

We saw in passing the Bible's call to wives to be submissive to their husbands. When the marriage celebrant says these words many a woman's heart is filled with dread, and some men's with glee. But this is a misunderstanding of what the Bible teaches.

> Submit to each other out of fear of Christ. Wives, submit to your own husbands, as to the Lord. For the husband is the head of the wife even as Christ is the head of the church, his body, and is himself its Saviour. Now as the church submits to Christ, so also wives should submit in everything to their husbands. Husbands, love your wives, as Christ loved the church and gave himself up for her, that he might sanctify her, having cleansed her by the washing of water with the word, so that he might present the church to himself in splendour, without spot or wrinkle or any such thing, that she might be holy and without blemish. (Ephesians 5.21-27)

This passage stands here as a separate paragraph. In fact, it is part of a long sentence (from verse 18) which begins by telling us to be full of the Spirit (rather than getting drunk). It goes on to tell us how: by singing, being thankful – and submitting to one another. The case of husbands and wives follows as an example of submission, but is still part of the same sentence. Later the cases of parents and children, and slaves and masters are dealt with.

"Submit to each another" doesn't mean husband and wife should each be equally submissive. The examples Paul gives are of up-down relationships, such as between a driver and a traffic policeman, or a pastor and his people. In all such relationships the Christian should be respectful of the authority of the one placed above them.

Marriage is modelled on the relationship of God with his people, and of Christ with his Church. These are ordered relationships. Christ is king of his community: he loves us, died for us, and lives again to bring us to perfection and happiness. The Son of God willingly submits to his Father's primacy. The true Church delights in Christ's salvation and willingly and joyfully accepts his leadership.[5]

The Greek word *hypotassomai*, is best translated as "subordinate yourself" (to someone), and means to voluntarily accept their leadership. In many areas of life and in most groups of people there are leaders and leadership structures. Sometimes leadership is forced on us (a dictator, a policeman), sometimes we choose it and cooperate with it willingly (the captain of a sporting team). The important thing to notice in our passage is that when Paul speaks of submission, he is speaking to women, not men. Nowhere does he counsel men to *make* their wives submit. His word to men is to *love* their wives, and the model he places before them is Jesus.

The family is a societal structure, which in Christian understanding has a leader. Decisions have to be made, sometimes hard ones. Always it is best to have consensus. Happy is the family where mother, father and children are always in agreement. But sometimes they are not, and there are occasions (hopefully not many) when a protocol is required to keep the family intact. Wives are encouraged to cooperate with and encourage the leadership of their husband in the family, and children likewise are counselled to obey their parents. The authoritarian husband who exploits this and lays a heavy burden on his wife, will probably destroy his family. His leadership should be sensitive and compassionate, and for the sake of the whole family; not for getting his own way. It is for the same reason that he is told not to aggravate his children.

But shouldn't there be equality between men and women? Many see this as an ideal. But it is important to understand that there are no two things in the universe that are absolutely equal. When we speak of equality we must always clarify what kind of equality we are seeking. Equality before the law means that male and female will receive equal treatment. We may also have the same rights when it comes to voting or serving in political office. Equal pay for equal work may be a good social policy. But men and women are not equal when it comes to their ability to bear a child, or breast-feed it, or to dig out a cesspit, or to play contact sports. It is true that women now play rugby, but not in the same teams as men. Women now serve in the military, but are given different tasks. The Bible sometimes assumes, and at times teaches, that men and women will play different roles in marriage. Many today can see no sense in this, see it as devaluing women, and dismiss it as belonging to an earlier age. Against this we must say that it does make sense, it gives women high value, and it is a teaching for all times. A couple who wish to please God and to have his blessing on their marriage will take it seriously.

We do not know all of the ways that God has made us different. Physical differences are obvious; minds are more complex. We may be sure that God's instructions will accord with the way he has made us, and with the future he intends. This is because we know him to be a good and righteous God. His law is for our happiness and the wellbeing of society. When Peter tells husbands to "live considerately" with their wives, "bestowing honour on the woman as the weaker sex", he acknowledges a God-created difference. When he adds that they are "joint-heirs of the grace of life", he marks an important equality. When he also adds, "in order that your prayers may not be hindered", he expresses the wish that husband and wife be a co-operative and effective praying team. We should keep in mind that Peter's listeners were part of a society in which the law gave very little protection to women against the bad behaviour of husbands. The desire of a husband to follow God was the best protection a wife could have. It may not be too different today. Important as police and courts may be, they are a clumsy instrument, for an already broken family. Better one should never need to go there.

Western societies are pursuing their own dream-future without regard for God's Word. Whether the outcome is what they desire is another thing. There is much wringing of hands and many public statements about violence in the home. It does not seem to have got less. The remedy, we are told, is greater equality, but that does not seem to have worked yet. Men do not refrain from fighting men because they are equal. Quite the opposite; they assume equality and fight for position, or their own way. Who is to say the modern insistence on equality may not be throwing some couples into a power struggle and adding to domestic violence? Unhappiness in the home can be the result of leadership struggles. Most men enter marriage wanting to please their wives, and wives their husbands. Selfishness sets in later. If a husband wants to insist he is leader, or a wife that she is equal, there will be friction. If, on the other hand, the husband seeks to love his wife and work for the family, and if she encourages him to take a lead and respects his leadership, there is a greater chance of harmony. Many men are confused about their roles. Confusion can lead to frustration, and frustration sometimes boils over into violence. One area in which this can work well is family prayers, when the family can consciously welcome God's presence, read his word and bring its needs to him. This is an area in which a husband can take a lead, though it is also a time for cooperation and sharing.

The Bible establishes a protocol for making difficult decisions. The husband is called on to lead, and the wife to accept his leadership. The husband is pointed to Christ as his model, and told to love his wife as Christ loves his Church. This means he will avoid selfish decision-making and seek to serve his wife. When the final decision is against her best judgement, she is counselled to respect her husband and encourage his leadership. The Christian husband, on the other hand, will see himself as the protector and perfecter of his wife. He will want her to be everything she can be, and will not take kindly to those who would demean her.

• • •

CHRISTIAN FAMILY

Same-Sex Attraction

How should Christians view homosexual people and practices? These are two quite different issues, and I raise them both, because "the single" today will often be suspected of being "gay"; thirty years ago such a thought would never have entered people's minds.

Christians should be respectful of same-sex attracted people as they should be of anyone. But this does not mean they are happy about "gay sex". The Bible consistently warns us against the practice of sodomy.

> Or do you not know that the unrighteous will not inherit the kingdom of God? Do not be deceived: neither the sexually immoral, nor idolaters, nor adulterers, nor men who practice homosexuality, nor thieves, nor the greedy, nor drunkards, nor revilers, nor swindlers will inherit the kingdom of God. And such were some of you. But you were washed, you were sanctified, you were justified in the name of the Lord Jesus Christ and by the Spirit of our God. (1 Corinthians 6.9-11)

Two men having anal sex is a twisting of what God made sex for. The strength of the Bible's warnings against sodomy point both to the attraction of the practice to some, and its danger. It was very common amongst the early Greeks and later the Romans, though not among the Jews, whose culture had been formed by the laws of Moses.[6] Many of those who heard the gospel and turned from their sins had practised sodomy. The Greek original of 1 Corinthians 6.9 - "nor men who practice homosexuality" – actually refers to two different practices. There is the *malakos* ("effeminate person") who plays the receptive role in the same-sex liaison, and the *arsenokoites* (male sex partner), who plays the male role. These cultural designations show how prevalent homosexual activity was in a Greek city like Corinth. The fact that such behaviour, unrepented, and continued, bars a person from the kingdom of God means that churches must never condone it, or cease to warn of its danger, just as they must teach against adultery, idolatry and greed.

The Christian attitude towards the *homosexual person* is a different question. In fact, there is no such word and no such concept in the Bible. "Homosexuality" is a word that was coined only one hundred and fifty years ago in the context of the newly developing field of psychiatry. It described a psychological "inversion", which most people who approached a psychotherapist wanted to be rid of. It is listed as a psychiatric condition in the first *Diagnostic and Statistical Manual of Mental Disorders* of 1952 (DSM1). Under pressure from gay activists it was removed from subsequent editions, and homosexuality came to be seen as either a normal condition some people are born with, or a life choice. Gay activists have neatly turned the tables on their former enemies and now refer to anyone who thinks that sodomy is wrong as "homophobic", as though having a moral objection indicates a mental disorder.

Being clear as to what we are talking about is important, for the debate over homosexuality in the church and in the public square is beset with misunderstanding. When orthodox Christians oppose homosexuality they are thinking of sodomy – and they want to be loyal to the Word of God. When liberal Christians and "forward-thinking" politicians defend it they speak of love: "What does it matter if two men or two women love one another? Doesn't Christianity teach love?" Words to this affect are repeated over and over. Two such radically different understandings of the one word are bound to lead to fruitless discussion.

Friendship between men can be very deep; the Greeks had a word for it, "brotherly love" (*philadelphia*), from which Paul dissociates homosexual relationships. Women too form deep friendships. Circumstances may well lead people to live together. This is good. In the past such behaviour would not have been seen as homosexual. It is a tragic modern confusion that people in need of simple community can be branded this way. "It is not good for the man to be alone." For one reason or another and at one time or another a man may not be sexually attracted to women, and live with another man. This does not make him "gay". Equally, a woman may have suffered badly at the hands of men, and find her companionship with another woman. This does not make her lesbian. Again, sadly, such people will be schooled to think of themselves as so, and encouraged to think they should be having sex.

As for the person who is drawn sexually to another person of the same gender, we need to state frankly that this is "unnatural". But it is important to explain that when Christians speak of something as "unnatural", they do not mean that it does not occur in nature, but that it is contrary to the way God has created human nature. Paul makes it clear that once we lose a knowledge of God we can be deceived into thinking anything is natural.

> For although they knew God, they did not honour him as God or give thanks to him, but they became futile in their thinking, and their foolish hearts were darkened. Claiming to be wise, they became fools, and exchanged the glory of the immortal God for images resembling mortal man and birds and animals and creeping things. Therefore, God gave them up in the lusts of their hearts to impurity, to the dishonouring of their bodies among themselves, because they exchanged the truth about God for a lie and worshiped and served the creature rather than the Creator, who is blessed forever! Amen. For this reason, God gave them up to dishonourable passions. For their women exchanged natural relations for those that are contrary to nature; and the men likewise gave up natural relations with women and were consumed with passion for one another, men committing shameless acts with men and receiving in themselves the due penalty for their error. (Romans 1.21-27)

Paul teaches us to expect homosexual confusion as a by-product of a society which turns its back on the knowledge of God. By calling these desires "unnatural" he does not mean that they don't happen, nor that in certain settings they may not be common. Nor does he mean that parallels cannot be found in the animal kingdom. When we call homosexuality unnatural we mean that it is contrary to what God teaches us is the meaning of sex. This does not mean that we discriminate against the person with these leanings, but we would counsel them not to indulge their desires. This may seem cruel, but is it any less cruel than to insist that those who feel strong sexual attraction to children control themselves and do what is right? We should expect to have people in our churches, who are struggling with homosexual and heterosexual issues; some may be afflicted with strong sexual feelings towards children. The congregation should be instructed that we are all sinners. Churches should not exclude anyone who is honestly trying to live in God's way. There should be places where people can talk openly and be encouraged to live in a Christian way.

The reason for including these reflections in a book on Christian marriage is because of our children. In the midst of the confusion of modern society children are at risk. School teachers may be afraid to present marriage and family as normal. "Gay" may be openly promoted, while to speak up for marriage and family could be labelled "homophobic". Teenage boys and girls driven by normal sexual feelings and at the most confusing moment in their adolescent development may be unwittingly subjected to grooming in the name of "political correctness". It happens very simply: shyness with the opposite sex, encouragement to experiment, then, if a boy happens to enjoy the act of sodomy, he will be told he is gay (or bisexual), and, when he is of age, there is a community waiting to welcome him, and reinforce his new identity. But in the normal course of growing up he would probably soon have outgrown his same-sex feelings and gone on to live a full and well-adjusted life.

These things need to be talked about in the family and in the church. Children need to grow up with a concept of normality and with models. Does normality mean "homophobia" (we should challenge this term), or hatred of "gays"? Absolutely not! The open parading of "gayism" in our world means inevitably that we will have friends, business acquaintances, teachers, and celebrities openly identifying themselves this way. We can respect them, associate with them and love them, though always reserving the right to explain, when challenged, that sodomy is sin, because the Bible says it is.

Many families now face the issue of one of their members "coming out". An adult son, for example, declares to his mother and father that he is "gay" and moves in with his male partner. How are parents and siblings to deal with this? Firstly, we cannot compromise on our faith in the Word of God, and ignore its warnings that to embrace a life of sin cuts us off from God and disqualifies us from his kingdom. So, we need to say that sodomy is sin. But the *friendship* enjoyed by these two men may be a fine and good thing, and there is no cause that we should look down on it. Similarly with two women. I have avoided the subject of lesbianism, mainly because the Bible says so little about it. It is only once mentioned - in the passage above - as an example of the confusion that results when people reject the knowledge of God. But for two women to be driven together by circumstances, or drawn together by deep affection, to share a home, even for life, is entirely honourable and should never draw a "lesbian" identity label. That schoolgirls should be groomed to think that because they go through a time of loving another girl, they are therefore "lesbian" is simply horrid. The challenge to the Christian family and the Christian church is to teach and model an attractive lifestyle that is consistent with the Word of God.

Divorce

This is an issue where Christians have different views. In what follows I am indebted to Ward Powers study, *Marriage and Divorce: The New Testament Teaching*.[7] We have seen how divorce is contrary to God's purpose for marriage. One thing we have not considered is the covenant involved, both in marriage and in our relationship with God. In the passage we have already looked at Malachi berates his countrymen in these words:

> And this second thing you do. You cover the LORD's altar with tears, with weeping and groaning because he no longer regards the offering or accepts it with favour from your hand. But you say, "Why does he not?" Because the LORD was witness between you and the wife of your youth, to whom you have been faithless, though she is your companion and your wife by covenant. (Malachi 2.13-14)

Marriage involves a covenant. A covenant is a solemn promise, enacted in some formal way, witnessed and publicly recorded. The man and woman promise each other that they will be faithful to each other for life; they vow to stick together through good times and bad; they will not go off with another partner. This is one aspect of Christian marriage, which happily has not yet been challenged by our secularizing world; even a civil marriage has at its heart the making of a covenant. This is one reason why *de facto* marriages are defective, even though real. A true marriage involves the making of a formal covenant, witnessed by others. When a man or woman simply live together it is not clear to others whether their relationship is honourable or sinful. For all our desire to be as inclusive as possible, a wise church will withhold communicant membership from a couple who are living together unmarried, until they regularize their partnership. Otherwise it becomes impossible for children in the church to have a clear view of the difference between marriage and immorality. A *de facto* partnership may have a solemn promise between the partners as its foundation, but unless it is declared in some way, it is not for others to know whether it is intended as a short term affair, or something more serious.

The covenant of marriage mirrors God's relationship with his people. Believers in Jesus live in covenant relationship with God. The covenant made at the time of Moses is no longer in force, but God has made a new one – different because it involves forgiveness and the gift of the Holy Spirit.[8]

When the Israelites came to Mt Sinai God entered into a covenant with them to be their God, and they his people – permanently. The covenant was enacted ceremonially and recorded for perpetuity. Of course, there were conditions, the most important of these being faithfulness, expressed in obedience to the law. God would not play false with Israel and they would not disobey him and go off after other gods. The Bible constantly celebrates God's covenant loyalty (*hesed*), but Israel sadly failed to honour its side of the agreement. God was forgiving to them again and again, but in the end he "divorced" them. This is a big part of the story of the Hebrew Scriptures.

We learn two things here. One is that divorce is abhorrent to God, the other is that sometimes it is necessary. In the Old Testament God acknowledges that divorce may take place "because of the uncleanness of a thing".[9] This expression was debated in the time of Jesus as though it were a proviso. Did it mean a man could divorce his wife if she displeased him in *any* way, or did it refer to serious sexual sin? Rabbi Hillel said that a man could divorce his wife even if she burned his food; Rabbi Shammai said only for serious sexual sin. These were opinions. The reality was that anyone could divorce his wife for any reason simply by serving her with a written notice (so no one could later accuse her of adultery), and repaying her dowry. When Jesus was asked for his opinion he intimated that for a man or woman to divorce and marry someone else (the most common reason for divorce) was tantamount to adultery; it was legal, but contrary to the spirit of the law.[10] When they asked him to explain why "Moses" (the law of God) allowed it, he said it was "for your hardness of heart". This means they were wrong to read it as a proviso ("you may divorce, in the following circumstances"); it was rather an acknowledgment of the reality of a broken situation. Our hardness of heart is such that divorce will sometimes occur. The intention of Moses' law was to forbid a woman returning to her former husband after she had become another man's wife.

Christians have often understood Jesus to mean that the old law is done away with, and a stricter law – no divorce – is enacted with the gospel. But this is not so. It would be the only case of Jesus replacing a moral law of the Old Testament with a new one. More likely is it that Jesus also acknowledges the broken human situation, and that his much-debated exception ("except for adultery"), is similarly not a proviso, but an acknowledgement of reality. The precise word he uses is not "adultery" (*moicheia*), though it is often misunderstood that way, but *porneia*, which is a much more general term.

If this is correct, Jesus is not forbidding divorce (he doesn't), nor even remarriage in every situation. Rather he makes it clear that to abandon your partner for someone else, even if it is done legally, is to commit adultery.

But there are situations where separation is unavoidable. A woman ought not to live with a man who is a habitually drunk and beats her, nor should a man or woman stay with a partner who is a habitual adulterer. Sometimes it is more loving to move out, than to support a partner who is wallowing in disgraceful conduct. Adultery violates the marriage covenant, as does physical abuse. A person may forgive an act of unfaithfulness, or even an affair, as God did with Israel, but they have every right to terminate the marriage, if such behaviour goes on. Only, we must take special care that we are not lured into divorce by the prospect of another relationship. That would be adultery. Jesus even mentions the case of a man who is waiting to marry a woman as soon as she can be free of her husband.[11] That too is adultery.

Divorce is extreme. It shatters the family, which is intended by God to reflect his faithfulness. He hates divorce. But there are circumstances in our troubled world when it will happen. At a later time, unconnected and distanced from the breakdown, if a divorced person remarries, it is not sin. "It is not good for man to be alone", and "it is better to marry than to burn". But a separated or divorced person must be careful. They will probably experience severe deprivation, and the feeling of need for another partner can be acute. It is most unwise to enter into a romantic partnership in the shadow of a broken marriage. A marriage entered into this way will find itself lumbered with the baggage of the past. Marriages like this mostly do not do well. You are well advised to put at least three years between a marriage breakup and contracting into a new one.

A divorced person should also consider the possibility of reconciliation. Divorce on it own is not necessarily the end of a marriage. It is only when a new marriage is contracted that the break becomes truly irreconcilable.

5
FINAL WORD

Families are the fundamental building block of society. Weaken the family and you weaken both the individual and the societies we live in. Yet, ever since Plato in his "Republic" theorized that the state should control the development of its ruling elite at the expense of the family, there have been those who have wanted to destroy the family in favour of some alternative system of control. Wherever it has been tried it has proved disastrous and abandoned. But people still wish to do it again.

Of course, the family sometimes fails. We can understand that someone who has suffered abuse at the hands of their family or a family member might question its value and wish for a better way. But there *is* no better way, and failures should not deter us from declaring the family's value and setting it forth as an ideal. If we do not – if we do not model functional family life and teach each new generation how to do it - we pave the way for more failures and more unhappiness.

Aloneness is where I began. Family enables us not to be alone, to have an identity, and for there always to be somewhere to come home to. In this age of human rights the right to belong to a family should be unquestioned. The ideal – and for many it is a reality – is father and mother and brothers and sisters. But I met children in India who as babes had been rescued from rubbish bins and taken to a mission. They had no father or mother or brother or sister, but were placed in a family-like group where they grew up with all these things, until a marriage was arranged and they left their mission home to start their own. And many flourished. In Ecuador I met a retired bishop and his wife who had forty children in addition to their three grown-up daughters. "Bishop, where did you get these children," we asked. He told us he got them from prisons, where mothers are forced to take their baby with them, but where there is danger for the child as it grows. A prison warder would beg him to take the child away before it suffered harm. The bishop's home was a happy community of "father", "mother", and "siblings" of all ages, where a child could grow up loved, until its birth family was able to reclaim it - or it could choose to leave. Or when it came of age he or she could marry and begin their own family. In Africa many children are parentless because of AIDS, but grandparents have taken them in and they have grown up in a family of sorts.

Churches can be strongholds of family life and values. Ministers should realize that not all have had the same advantages of modelling and teaching. *Teach* about marriage, singleness, parenting, family Bible-reading and prayers, special occasions and so on. *Invite* a mother to share about her mothering, a father about his fathering, and single aunts and uncles to teach and share their skills. *Encourage* families to do things together – and do not leave out the singles! Point church members to good books! Arrange family events in the church; make use of the great festivals.

The church congregation is a community of families, and powerful in a good way. I think of one of my children coming home from school having realized for the first time that not everyone believes in Jesus, and wondering whether Mum and Dad were odd. On Sunday he is greeted by another father in the congregation, who always takes notice of him, whom he respects and loves. "He is a Christian too," my son thinks, "so Mum and Dad may be *different*, but they are not weird" – there is a bigger family, a Christian family, to which we all belong.

Then there was the child from a non-Christian home, who would often go to breakfast at her friend's house, where her friend's Mum and Dad were Christians and read the Bible and prayed at the meal table. That was how she came to know God as her real Father and the Lord Jesus as her Saviour. Families should be inclusive; they should spill over into hospitality. Whenever I pray for a newborn child, among many things, I ask God that he or she should grow up to know the God who has given them life, and the Saviour who has died to give them eternal life … and that they should become a light to others and a rock of stability and love in a world of confusion and hate.

One could go on telling stories. It is my hope that this book might lead to much discussion about marriage, raising children, being raised as a child, and being family – and the telling of many stories.

***

A Story

My eldest daughter, Ruth, went from South Africa to a gap year in Scotland. She joined a church which practised "believers' baptism", so was encouraged to be rebaptized. She considered this and decided against it. Later, her Bible Study group decided they would all write out their stories, read them to each other, and then go "witnessing" in the streets. They would use their stories in conversation. Here is Ruth's story. I am grateful to that church for accepting her as "an exception to the rule". In every church there will be exceptions. They accepted her as she was, trained her, and used her in their ministry team. And she grew!

My Testimony

I was born in Perth, Australia in 1985 - the second child of a minister and his wife. My parents chose to baptize me as a baby because they believed, and still do, that in accepting *them* into his family God also accepted *all their children*. We were a Christian family and my parents believed that the covenant promises belonged to me as well as them. Had I died as an infant I would have been saved, as I belonged to Jesus.

Their reading of the Bible encouraged them to think that this is how the early Christians thought and acted. One cannot prove from the New Testament that they baptized their children, but it looks like they did and it is consistent with the Old Testament practice of circumcising children. (Acts 2:39, Mk 10:13-16, Acts 16:31)

I know this raises many questions: Was I born again? (probably not) Is it possible I could reject Christ later on and be lost? (probably). Nevertheless, my parents firmly believed this is the way God wants us to understand ourselves as a family in Him.

So, they taught me to think of God as my Father and Jesus as my Saviour, even though I was too young to have made any decision. They asked the church family to accept me as a member of the church and to treat me as a Christian sister. At that young age - because it made sense to my parents that God treats the family as one in this way - they sought to encourage me in *relationship* with God, not convert me.

Therefore, when I am asked the question "when did you become a Christian?" it is difficult to say, because I can never remember a time when I didn't speak to Jesus and have a relationship with him and believe in him.

But also, of course, in time my parents had to teach me that it was necessary for me to have my own faith in Jesus. It was part of the natural growing process that somewhere in adolescence I would develop an independent mind and judgement. I might reject the faith that was chosen for me and even renounce my baptism, or I might decide to own it and confirm it in whatever way.

When I was 7 years old (in 1992) my parents made a decision (after consistent and thoughtful prayer) on behalf of the whole family to move to South Africa. My dad had been asked to become the principal of George Whitefield Theological College, which educates men and women in the knowledge of God and trains them for a variety of Christian ministries.

My older brother, two younger sisters, and I were enrolled in a school 5 minutes' walk down the road from our house and our family began to integrate into our new phase of life, with mum devoting her all to supporting all of our needs (a tough job in a family of 6).

Our move to South Africa was met with fear from a lot of people back home in Australia, especially because we moved there in a time of uncertainty the year before the elections of 1994, when no-one knew how peaceful or otherwise the presidential election of Nelson Mandela would be. God's mercy was with us then and always has been. We have been mercifully protected and blessed abundantly in his work. (Mark 10:29-31)

As I grew up I certainly must have been developing an independent mind and judgement, and when I was about 11 or 12 years old (leading up to my adolescence) I was really struck by a lesson my Sunday school teacher was trying to explain. My brother was mucking around but I was listening carefully and heard that I had to make an important decision in my life; to either

- live "my own way" (rejecting God and trying to rule my life without him), or

- live God's way (submitting to Jesus as my ruler and relying on his promise and power of salvation).

It was a very intense moment for me and I knew that I had the freedom to choose either option. We then had a moment to pray and I clearly remember whole-heartedly and fervently choosing to commit myself and my life to following Jesus! I confirmed my faith and acceptance of the gift of being a child of God!!

Throughout my life, God has been faithful in developing my maturity in Christ. My *spiritual* worship is presenting my *body* as a living sacrifice, holy and acceptable to God (Romans 12:1). I often fall short of this and I know that there will always be room for growth in my knowledge, discernment and actions. My hope and assurance comes from his word that ***I am saved*** because I have put my faith in Him, and "He who started a good work in me will carry it on to completion until the day of Christ Jesus" (Philippians 1:6).

NOTES

WHY I WROTE THIS BOOKLET

1. I was helped in this by Dr John Newby.

1. CHRISTIAN MARRIAGE

1. 1 Corinthians 11.12
2. Matthew 19.4-6
3. Malachi 2.13-16 (Hebrew; NIV)
4. Read the book of Hosea, especially chapters 1-3.
5. John 2.1-11
6. Mark 2.19-22

2. CHILDREN

1. Genesis 3.19
2. Ephesians 1.18-23; 1 Corinthians 5.3; Hebrews 2.5-9
3. Matthew 23.23
4. John 8.34
5. Jeremiah 31.31-34; Ezekiel 36.24-28
6. Romans 10.9-13
7. Luke 18.15. The word *brephos* means a foetus or a new born child.
8. John 3.16
9. Mark 2.15-17
10. John 3.1-10; Ephesians 2.1-10

3. THE CHRISTIAN FAMILY

1. Genesis 15.2-3
2. Genesis 16, 21
3. Luke 2.41-51
4. Matthew 1.16; Luke 3.23
5. Luke 2.51
6. Exodus 20.12
7. E.g. Proverbs 1.8-9; 6.20-21
8. To be convinced of the truth of this read Romans, Galatians and Ephesians. In Romans 4 Paul explains the relationship between faith, circumcision and salva-

NOTES

tion. His argument also covers baptism. It is a sign or seal of a salvation received by faith.
9. This is similar to what Paul argues of circumcision. Abraham believed and was justified prior to circumcision, which was "a seal of the righteousness he had by faith while he was still uncircumcised." (Romans 4.11)
10. John 3.8
11. Ephesians 6.4
12. For example, notice the way Paul exhorts Timothy and reminds him of the gospel in 2 Timothy 1.

4. FAMILY MATTERS

1. In Luke 14.26 Jesus demands of his disciples that they "hate" their nearest relations. His strong language makes sense if he had to reject ("hate") his own mother to go to the cross. That is, he had to treat her as though he hated her.
2. 1 Corinthians 7.1, 7, 25-31
3. Modern genetics has disproved the notion that mixing of bloodlines (ethnicities) leads to weakness. The opposite is the case.
4. 1 Corinthians 7.39
5. 1 Corinthians 11.3
6. The practice was not condoned in the early Roman period. It became common later due to the influence of the Greeks.
7. B. Ward Powers, *Marriage and Divorce: The New Testament Teaching*, Family Life & Jordan Books: Concord & Petersham,1987.
8. Jeremiah 31.31-34; Hebrews 8 - 10
9. Deuteronomy 24.1-4
10. Matthew 19.1-9
11. Luke 16.18

www.ingramcontent.com/pod-product-compliance
Lightning Source LLC
Chambersburg PA
CBHW021959290426
44108CB00012B/1133